"James Atwood has written a faith-based summons to act in hope, to refuse the collusion of despair, and to take faith seriously enough to make a difference. This book is urgent for all those who care about the future of our society and who are ready to act in informed ways."
—**WALTER BRUEGGEMANN**, PROFESSOR EMERITUS AT COLUMBIA THEOLOGICAL SEMINARY

"James Atwood knows that we have both a gun problem and a heart problem, and he addresses both. If you care about life, this is required reading."
—**SHANE CLAIBORNE**, ACTIVIST, AUTHOR, AND FOUNDER OF RED LETTER CHRISTIANS

"I recommend that congregations who feel hopeless and powerless in confronting gun violence in our society read *Collateral Damage* together. You will be inspired—and changed."
—**KATIE DAY**, CHARLES A. SCHIEREN PROFESSOR EMERITA OF CHURCH AND SOCIETY AT UNITED LUTHERAN SEMINARY IN PHILADELPHIA

"Trust this man and his words. He has researched them well. He has lived them. Then follow his lead and rise up. Peace and justice are God's work and ours, in collaboration. Together we can, in Atwood's words, 'work for God's peaceful tomorrow.'"
—**PHIL KNISS**, SENIOR PASTOR OF PARK VIEW MENNONITE CHURCH

"James Atwood makes a compelling argument that the conversation about firearms is indeed a moral one—and that the status quo is unacceptable. People of faith and all who want to leave a better world for their children should run to read this book."
—**PETER S. BERG**, SENIOR RABBI AT THE TEMPLE IN ATLANTA

"Speaking from deep faith and reverence for life, former missionary, pastor, peace activist, and responsible gun owner James Atwood calls all, especially the faithful, to help restore sanity and common-sense safety not only for the sake of the nation but for the sake of the gospel."
—**AL TIZON**, AFFILIATE ASSOCIATE PROFESSOR OF MISSIONAL AND GLOBAL LEADERSHIP AT NORTH PARK UNIVERSITY

"As a disaster psychologist, I have seen too often the significant, lasting, and largely overlooked 'collateral damage' of gun violence. With this sobering and ultimately hopeful book, James Atwood shows that the prevalence of gun violence is not just a safety crisis but also a spiritual one."
—**JAMIE ATEN**, BLANCHARD CHAIR OF HUMANITARIAN AND DISASTER LEADERSHIP AT WHEATON COLLEGE

COLLATERAL DAMAGE

COLLATERAL DAMAGE

Changing the Conversation about Firearms and Faith

JAMES E. ATWOOD

HERALD PRESS

Harrisonburg, Virginia

Herald Press
PO Box 866, Harrisonburg, Virginia 22803
www.HeraldPress.com

Library of Congress Cataloging-in-Publication Data
Names: Atwood, James E., author.
Title: Collateral damage : changing the conversation about firearms and faith
/ James E. Atwood.
Description: Harrisonburg : Herald Press, 2019. | Includes bibliographical
references.
Identifiers: LCCN 2019015991| ISBN 9781513804866 (pbk. : alk. paper)
| ISBN 9781513804873 (hardcover : alk. paper)
Subjects: LCSH: United States—Church history—21st century. | United
States—Social conditions. | Violence—Religious aspects—Christianity. |
Firearms—Religious aspects—Christianity. | Firearms—United States.
Classification: LCC BR526 .A89 2019 | DDC 363.330973—dc23 LC record
available at https://lccn.loc.gov/2019015991

COLLATERAL DAMAGE
© 2019 by Herald Press, Harrisonburg, Virginia 22803. 800-245-7894.
All rights reserved.
Library of Congress Control Number: 2019015991
International Standard Book Number: 978-1-5138-0486-6 (paperback);
978-1-5138-0487-3 (hardcover); 978-1-5138-0488-0 (ebook)
Printed in United States of America
Cover and interior design by Merrill Miller

23 22 21 20 19   10 9 8 7 6 5 4 3 2 1

*Dedicated to all those who
work for justice and live in hope for
God's tomorrow*

CONTENTS

Foreword

W E HAVE A serious crisis in the United States with regard to our valuing of human life. Our nation is a place of extreme violence, leading to nearly forty thousand deaths per year caused primarily by the use of guns. As Jim Atwood writes in these pages, these tragic deaths are just one form of the collateral damage wrought by gun violence. Families suffer. Children are traumatized by school lockdown drills and growing up in neighborhoods plagued by violence. Survivors of gun violence carry physical and psychological wounds. The economic cost of medical care, security measures, and loss of life is staggering.

If this damage were not enough, we lack the will to do anything about this crisis. Gun deaths are so common in the United States that we are numb to the impact of guns on human life. Our newscasts report police shootings, neighborhood murders, school shootings, drive-by shootings, domestic shootings, night club shootings, shootings in houses of worship, suicides by guns, accidental shootings, shootings of children by other children; and the list of the various ways that we have devalued human life in the United States of America continues. It feels as though we have become a nation numb to the pain of a family losing a loved one to gun violence. Gun deaths are a seemingly acceptable norm in our culture. This epidemic is consistent with our obsession with violence and devaluing human life.

During the time I served as the director of the Presbyterian Church (USA) Office of Public Witness (2010–16), our denomination approved policy intended to provide an advocacy platform to reduce gun violence in the United States. At the time, gun-related deaths were nearly thirty thousand per year.[1] Admittedly, I was shocked at the enormity of this problem, although the news of gun violence even in my local community was at the top of the news hour each morning and evening. Immediately, our office moved to make eradicating gun violence a primary justice advocacy issue. This may have seemed like an overly ambitious goal, but the call to transform a violent culture into a remnant of the peaceable kin-dom is a radical and revolutionary effort.

Collateral Damage does not spare criticism of the National Rifle Association, nor should it. The NRA is a powerful lobby that influences many of the decisions our congressional leaders make with regard to easy access to guns. We witness the influence of this organization through the lens of weak U.S. gun laws. I was stunned to discover that gun lobbies had infused so much money into political campaigns that many of our congressional leaders were bound to support efforts to expand the sale of over-the-counter guns, including assault weapons (which are war weapons). These political contributions serve the gun industry well by securing congressional votes to maintain laws that give easy access to purchasing guns.

As I reflect on the compounded effects of the collateral damage of gun violence, I remember my first workshop on reducing gun violence after our denominational policy was approved. It was eight months after the Sandy Hook Elementary School shooting. I was invited to return to my home state of South

Carolina to offer a workshop. Given the congressional stalling and dismissal of this tragic event, it seemed to be a reasonable opportunity to broach the discussion. After all, I was in my home state with friends and colleagues who shared relational connections to my family and collegial relationships that dated back to seminary days.

The educational room was about three-quarters full. Just a few minutes into my presentation, the interruptions began. It was clear that many people were upset that the topic was being discussed. Some felt that the workshop was promoting an anti-gun sentiment. Also, the theme resonated across the room that I was trying to take their guns. Neither of these assessments was accurate. I had only come to bring awareness to the pervasive nature of gun violence in our nation and its heavy death toll.

During the exchanges, I noticed a group of about six women sitting together. They had been listening intently to the discussion while comforting each other continually. One or two occasionally wiped away tears. I found an opening to invite them into the discussion.

These women explained that they were part of the same congregation. They were in pain over a recent occurrence of gun violence that led to the death of a teenager in their community. One of them explained that she had moved from one part of the county to another that was deemed safer, both statistically and economically. However, their collective sadness was evident through their tears. The woman went on to say that none of them had imagined that the posh community they lived in would face a tragedy that would put them in a position of having to comfort the parents of a teenager in their congregation who had killed another youth with a rented gun.

The woman said that the gun rental would have cost the teen $75. But because he turned it in late it cost $150. They were shocked that he had even been able to rent a gun. A pall hung over the discussion. Then an elder who had argued throughout the workshop said, "Well, if it takes any longer for me to get a gun in the state of South Carolina than it does now, I will just have to find another way to get one."

This cold retort from a well-educated officer of the church brings to mind Jim Atwood's earlier writings, which express the deep idolatry that accompanies the proliferation of guns as symbols of power. I want to suggest that the need for more and more guns is a symbol of our distance from our Creator, because it symbolizes our weakness in learning more deeply how to love. However, one can only understand this view if love is the epitome of one's understanding of the core of an eternal being.

I am grateful for the many years Jim Atwood has devoted to preventing gun violence, and for his books that have inspired the faith community to action. I am grateful too that *Collateral Damage* addresses the issue of race and racism and the impact on the epidemic of gun violence within the African American community. I am all too familiar with the economic disparities that drive personal and financial insecurities while creating deep wells of barren hopes for poor people in the United States. My wife and I chartered a congregation in the Presbyterian Church (USA) that intentionally evangelized people who are poor in Memphis, Tennessee, and it is abundantly clear that the constant desperation among poor people, particularly African Americans, is a result of internalized oppression caused by historical and current marginalization in this country. To ignore this historical and current reality is to dehumanize the entire African American community while ignoring the historic evil at the root of such high rates of gun violence in the African American community. Currently, our government is not understanding this reality. We will not remedy the problem of gun violence in the African American community without an economic solution.

It must also be mentioned that as more new immigrants come into this country as economically marginalized citizens, we stand to see an even greater increase in violence by guns. The same marginalization, deprivation, and despair that has occurred historically with African Americans is bound to happen with other groups who find themselves in the throes of stagnant means of living. For some, criminality may seem the only means of feeding their families. Gun violence, like poverty, does not operate in a vacuum.

Our elected leaders must take seriously the human need to have a meaningful and productive life. I believe that this is drawn from the wells of our Creator's love for all of creation. It is imperative that we focus on broadening our love for one another while seeking to build a fabric of hope that embraces more than just a few. We may then have a chance to end gun violence and prevent its collateral damage.

—Rev. Dr. J. Herbert Nelson II
Stated Clerk of the General Assembly
of the Presbyterian Church (USA)

1

NOT IN THE STATS
The Collateral Damage of 393 Million Guns

O**NE HUNDRED PEOPLE DIE** from gun violence every day in the United States. Some fifty children and teens are shot each day. Nearly forty thousand people died at the barrels of revolvers and other firearms in 2017. Since 1979, more Americans have been killed by guns in our cities and towns than all service members slain on the battlefields of all our wars since 1775.[1]

Three hundred and ninety-three million: that is the current estimate as to how many guns we have in the United States. That's more than one gun for every man, woman, and child. There are 120.5 guns for every hundred residents of the United States—almost twice the firearm ownership rate of the next-highest country, Yemen, with about 52 guns per hundred residents.[2] In 2016, U.S. gun companies manufactured a record 11 million firearms, up from the approximate 6.5 million firearms manufactured in 2011. That is an estimated 69 percent increase in firearms manufactured in the United States within the last five years. We imported another 5.1 million firearms in 2016, a 30 percent increase from 2015.[3]

The number of firearms in the United States has risen sharply (see figure below). One needn't be a statistician to predict that in a few short years we will have a half billion guns in the country. Nor does it require clairvoyance to realize these vast numbers of firearms will inevitably result in more suicides, homicides, murder-suicides, suicides by cop, incidents of domestic violence, police shootings, school shootings, mall shootings, cases of children shooting children, accidental shootings, shootings during the commission of a crime, and gang-related shootings. What category am I missing?

Let's be clear: other than a starter pistol for track and field, most guns are made to kill. Gun aficionados may claim other exceptions, such as personalized shotguns for skeet shooting or other sport shooting firearms. But *any* gun can maim or kill when a human being becomes a target. Hundreds of millions of guns, capable of taking a human life in an instant, put our entire

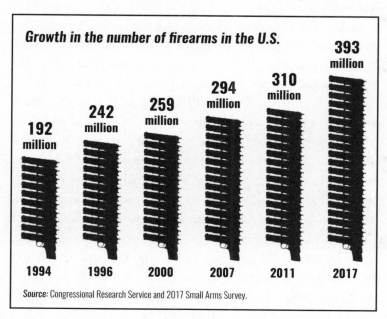

Growth in the number of firearms in the U.S.

192 million — 1994
242 million — 1996
259 million — 2000
294 million — 2007
310 million — 2011
393 million — 2017

Source: Congressional Research Service and 2017 Small Arms Survey.

country at risk. If it is true that each gun is made to kill, these statistics suggest they are doing their job quite well.

A steady rise in suicides involving firearms has pushed the rate of gun deaths in the United States to its highest in more than twenty years. In 2017, according to new figures from the Centers for Disease Control and Prevention, 39,773 people in the United States lost their lives at the point of a gun. When adjusted for age fluctuations, "that represents a total of 12 deaths per 100,000 people—up from 10.1 in 2010. . . . What that bare statistic represents in terms of human tragedy is most starkly reflected when set alongside those of other countries." According to a recent study published in the *Journal of the American Medical Association*, that "compares with rates of 0.2 deaths per 100,000 people in Japan, 0.3 in the United Kingdom, 0.9 in Germany, and 2.1 in Canada."[4]

Whenever there is a mass shooting in the United States, those who die get the headlines. But the family members, friends, and acquaintances left behind are long-term victims. Like a pebble dropped into a quiet pond, death ripples outward, expanding to the farthest shore. Those ripples reach not only dozens but hundreds and even thousands of others. For the rest of their lives, the survivors must deal with broken hearts. The deceased had parents, siblings, children, cousins, and aunts and uncles and grandparents who loved them. There are friends and business colleagues, church friends, neighbors, and the crew who met for bowling every Thursday night. Their lives will never be the same.

Death leaves a hole that can never be filled, even by a multitude of other relationships. Each victim was a valued member of a community. If she belonged to a church, the congregation knows where she sat. His Sunday school class is not the same anymore. If he coached a Little League baseball team or attended basketball camp or read to the visually impaired, or if she played in a band or chaired the board of a local non-profit or was part of a book club: the loss of this person affects hundreds of people. The survivors cannot forget how one of their own was murdered. Office colleagues are reminded daily of the violence that took away one of their coworkers. Teachers remember the child who wanted to be a teacher or a doctor or a basketball player. When the one killed was the breadwinner for a household, the financial losses pile on top of the emotional ones. Survivors of each victim miss the one whose life was snuffed out, and they think about how the person died. And they often wonder if they might face a similar fate.

Guns, gunshots, and gun deaths are becoming a way of life for millions of us. You could write a book about each victim of gun violence—but you would have to write forty thousand books in one year. You could write a book that summarizes the stories of all these victims, outlining in its pages the life of each person killed by gun violence in one year. That would be a massive tome.

But here's the thing: those who are killed or maimed by guns aren't the only victims. We must confront not only the indiscriminate killing of infants, toddlers, youth, and adults but also the collateral damage in terms of the indescribable heartaches of the families and friends whose loved ones have been killed, injured, or simply shot at. The primary focus of *Collateral Damage* is the byproduct of living in the presence of 393 million guns. We must talk about those who died, and also about their loved ones and friends who face great trauma.

If you were a reporter investigating a nuclear meltdown, you would likely try to get to ground zero. You would go as close as possible to the scene of the atomic reactor and report on the devastation you'd find at the epicenter. But you'd also want to visit those living within a radius of several hundred miles. You'd want to report on the fallout for all those impacted by the explosion, whether near or close at hand. Some of the consequences of the fallout would be immediately visible; some might be invisible, at least for a time. When an area has been affected by a nuclear disaster, you don't assume only those killed were affected. You assume there is collateral damage for everyone, near and far.

Collateral damage is "the unintended detrimental consequences of any action or decision."[5] Living in a society with more guns than people is a bit like living in an area where there has been a nuclear meltdown: the damage extends for miles around and stretches out for years into the future. Far more civilians die on our own streets than soldiers in combat. Our nation is in disaster mode.

List of casualties

The collateral damage of gun violence begins when people purchase a firearm, believing that they can now protect themselves and their loved ones from dangerous people. These guns, purchased for protection, are the very ones that often take the lives of those whom the purchasers most wanted to protect. Reputable research reveals that a gun bought to protect one's home from intruders is twelve times more likely to be used, intentionally or by accident, against a family member or other member of the household than to be used to stop an intruder.[6] That figure doesn't include other gun injuries or deaths, including suicides and criminal homicides involving stolen guns.

When one of God's children is killed, it is the end of that person's earthly life. Collateral damage is what happens next. Collateral damage is felt intensely by those closest to the victim. They face incalculable pain now that a precious loved one has been ripped away from their family circle and community. The loved one's place at the dinner table is now and forevermore an empty chair; their smile no longer lights up the room; they offer no more hugs and kisses; the tender "Good nights" are no more. We cannot place a monetary value on the loss of that one human life. It is beyond measure and beyond price. And while the victim's life may end in an instant, the victim's survivors will experience the loss forever. Yet these survivors of gun violence don't appear on any list of casualties.

Collateral damage also includes the profound sense of guilt that parents or caregivers feel when a loved one is assaulted or killed. They often repeatedly second-guess themselves. The questions keep recurring: "What could I have done differently?" "What if I had refused her permission to go to the party?" "Why didn't I tell him to come right home after the game?" Said one parent, "There are days when I struggle to get out of bed. It takes all my strength just to get up." As Claudius says to Gertrude in *Hamlet*, "When sorrows come, they come not as single spies, but in battalions."

The death of a child has long-term, life-changing effects on parents. A 2008 study published in the *Journal of Family Psychology* found that these effects include "more depressive symptoms, poorer well-being, and more health problems."[7] Given the unbelievable emotional toll of losing a child to gun violence, the strength displayed by parents who are immediately thrust into the public eye, and who are henceforth known as "activists," is immense.

But not all activists survive. Jeremy Richman fought the good fight for six years after his beautiful first-grade daughter, Avielle, was murdered along with twenty other children at Sandy Hook Elementary School. He and his wife established a foundation in their daughter's memory to promote research into the brain pathologies that lead to violence. Richman, a neuroscientist, was nationally known for his advocacy on mental health issues, and in 2015 he was given an appointment as a lecturer at Yale Medical School. But his psychological trauma was too great, and he took his own life in March 2019. He was forty-nine years old.[8] How would you describe his early death? I must call it collateral damage.

Those present at shootings, whether injured or not, live with some level of trauma and indescribable pain. At the one-year commemoration of the tragedy at Parkland, Florida, two high school students who survived the initial killing spree could no longer deal with their despair, and took their own lives. Not only our bodies but our minds bear the scars of confrontations with killing machines.

One of my friends, Colin Goddard, was shot four times in the 2007 Virginia Tech massacre. He fought valiantly for his life in intensive care for weeks and won the battle. He recovered to become a powerful messenger for sensible gun laws throughout the country. His body, however, carried four bullets that resulted in a severe case of lead poisoning ten years later. One of the bullets was lodged in his pelvis and required surgeons to break his hip to remove what was poisoning his blood. That meant another long and expensive period of recovery before Colin could walk normally again. He was shot ten years earlier, but the attack lingered on in his body as well as in his mind.

Colin is not alone. The thousands who are shot become the walking wounded, carrying bullets or bullet fragments wedged in their bodies that surgeons cannot safely remove. Some 95 percent of America's ammunition contains toxic lead. One surgeon calls lead poisoning in gunshot survivors "a huge problem, and I'm seeing it more and more. And if I'm just one physician seeing it more and more, it's just the tip of the iceberg."[9]

Lisa Hamp, another survivor of that 2007 mass shooting in Blacksburg, Virginia, is preoccupied about her safety everywhere she goes. She consciously chooses which seat in a coffee shop or restaurant would provide the best escape route. Her eyes scan everyone around her in a crowd as she looks for unusual behavior, and she can hear a pin drop.

"There are thousands like me, as well as law enforcement officers and medics," she writes. "These people may think for a long time that they weren't affected because the media doesn't mention them. They may have escaped gun wounds, but the mental wounds run deep. They walk around wounded for months, sometimes years before realizing the impact the shooting has had on them. It's a long road to recovery for everyone. When is enough, enough?"[10]

Children and youth may escape getting shot, but they cannot escape the lasting, poisonous effects of gun violence in their schools and neighborhoods. Nor can those living in many communities ignore the psychological trauma that comes from listening to gunshots in their neighborhood before they go to sleep at night or from hearing another story of an unarmed Black person being shot by police.

Epidemiologists tell us that the very presence of thousands of guns in a community has a detrimental effect on *all* its citizens. If there are guns around, sooner or later they will likely fire, on purpose or accidentally. The collateral damage will be immense and unmeasurable, and much of it will unfold over time.

We have known for some time that children and youth who live closest to acts of neighborhood violence have greater stress, longer bouts of depression, and a harder time learning than those who live in neighborhoods less plagued by gun violence. In Chicago, school choice policies enable students from many different neighborhoods to attend a single school. This prompted Julia Burdick-Will, a sociologist from Johns Hopkins University, to examine the effects of gun violence on students who live in a variety of neighborhoods. Her research revealed that *any* classmate's exposure to violence had a detrimental effect on *everyone* in the classroom, even those who lived a considerable distance away from the violence. Schools are increasingly recognizing trauma as a factor that derails the learning process to significant degrees.[11] Such trauma enforces the idea for these young people that the world is not a safe place. The effects are cumulative. Some children have trouble eating, others spend a lot of time in nurses' offices complaining of stomachaches and headaches.

Still others know the collateral damage from guns without a shot ever being fired. The daughter of a colleague of mine was mugged and had her car stolen by a gun-wielding assailant when she was a college student. Fifteen years have passed, but nightmares regularly stalk her sleep, especially after a mass shooting anywhere in the country. She continually relives that awful moment when she was accosted and forced to look down the barrel of a gun that could easily have taken her life. What do you call such fear? I call it collateral damage.

The American Psychological Association continually warns parents that the gunfights, murders, and explosions that our children watch daily on television and in video games and movies have an adverse effect on them. Current scholarship verifies the link between violent media and the development of aggressive behavior in all age groups. The sheer number of guns in our country increases incivility, a trust in violence, fear, and anxiety.

Despair and thoughts and prayers

One of the most frightening things about all this collateral damage—from the immediate losses suffered by families of victims to the generalized damage to culture at large—is that there's no sign of it abating anytime soon. Our laws are designed to protect the sale of more guns rather than protect the safety of our people. No other developed country in the world permits such carnage. But unless our citizens demand a change, the collateral damage brought on by ever-increasing numbers of firearms will only multiply.

In decades past, the faith community has responded to that reality by giving in to despair—a temptation for many. Some shake their heads and say, "All we can do is pray." And as we lament the latest mass shooting, we timidly assure the victims' families that they are "in our thoughts and prayers."

Having been deeply involved with fainthearted churches for more than four decades, I know well that kind of despair. But as a Christian, I refuse to *live* in what John Bunyan, in *The Pilgrim's Progress*, called "the Slough of Despond." On our Christian journeys, each of us has spent some time in that awful place, but by the grace of God we do not have to stay there. God does not call us to acquiesce to the power of evil but gives us a spirit of power to do battle against the forces of evil in our violent culture (see Ephesians 6:10-17).

Violence in any form is an affront to God and all that is good in any society. I say unequivocally: It is not God's will that one hundred of God's children are shot or killed every day.

The day gun violence hit home

My life as a young pastor, and the trajectory of my ministry, changed almost in the twinkling of an eye one afternoon in 1975. My secretary informed me I had a telephone call from the intensive care unit of a local hospital. One of my parishioners, Herb Hunter, had been shot. He was now at death's door.

Later I would hear the story—a story that still makes me livid. The teenager who shot Herb had complained to a friend at the local bowling alley that he had no money. His friend reached into his jacket and pulled out a Saturday night special, saying, "Here, go get yourself some money. And when you get some, give me twenty bucks and you can keep the gun." The teen went to the motel where Herb was working at the front desk and shot him. Herb died two days later from the gunshot wounds.

The day after his funeral, I drove into Washington, D.C., and volunteered my services to the Coalition to Stop Gun Violence. Everything else I was doing at the time no longer seemed relevant. Sitting on my couch and claiming that gun violence was a political matter and that preachers are not trained for such things: well, my Christian faith wouldn't allow me to get by with that nonsense. I had to *do* something. Preventing other families and churches from going through what we had gone through became my priority.

For the last forty-five years, I have been actively recruiting people of faith to work together to stop our nation's unique gun pandemic. I have done just about anything and everything I can think of to convince the church that America's greatest spiritual and moral crisis is the violence that comes from the barrels of unrestricted and unregulated guns. I've stuffed envelopes, served on boards, lobbied Congress and state representatives, written dozens of speeches and sermons and three resolutions which became policy for the Presbyterian Church (USA), authored three books; marched in demonstrations, and helped to coordinate the Million Mom March.

After I buried Herb, the Lord's Prayer I mouthed every Sunday took on increased clarity and urgency. As I led my congregation in Jesus' prayer that God's kingdom would come on earth as it is in heaven, I found myself convicted that Jesus' words demanded an increased commitment. Before my parishioner's death, I thought that the Lord's Prayer pertained more to God's victory at the end of recorded time. The kingdom might be coming, but it was still light-years away. After Herb was murdered, the Lord's Prayer became for me a call similar to that of Jeremiah's: to "seek the welfare of the city" in the here and now (Jeremiah 29:7). Today, when I pray that God's kingdom will come on earth as it is in heaven, I'm yearning for it *today*. I'm praying that God's peaceful tomorrow comes as soon as possible, because the Lord knows how tired we are of this violence.

I'll admit: sometimes it's hard not to get discouraged. In 1975, the year Herb was gunned down, over thirty-five thousand Americans were killed by firearms. In 2017, almost forty thousand precious sons and daughters were killed by guns.[12] That's not the direction we need these numbers to go.

If I thought that what little I have been able to do to prevent gun violence was of no consequence in the building of God's kingdom, I would quit this work in a heartbeat. But I am totally convinced of the trustworthiness of God's promise that our labor in the Lord is never, ever, in vain (1 Corinthians 15:58). I am betting my life that one day, justice will "roll down like waters, and righteousness like an ever-flowing stream" (Amos 5:24) and gun violence will be a thing of the past.

Debate, argue, and plead about the kingdom

You may be surprised to learn that, alongside my advocacy and activism against gun violence, I also enjoyed hunting for well over fifty years. Some of my most enjoyable days were spent deer hunting at Pinetop in Gore, Virginia, where my close friend Wil Johnson owned a tree farm. It was fun scouting the terrain for buck rubs and game trails and making a deer stand in hopes that a big-antlered buck would soon pay me a call.

So no one who loves his or her gun can call me a "gun grabber," as some are prone to do with anyone who advocates for sensible gun laws. As an octogenarian, I don't own hunting rifles anymore, but as a former hunter, I know that a love of hunting doesn't preclude a commitment to common-sense gun legislation. As we'll see in this book, more than 90 percent of Americans, including gun owners, support measures like universal background checks. There is so much common ground.

One of the most provocative Scripture passages I use in my work is Acts 19:8. It describes the apostle Paul's work in Ephesus: "He entered the synagogue and for three months spoke boldly, arguing and pleading about the kingdom of God." Now, if you know anything about the missionary journeys of Paul, you know that he got around! Every time the wind blew, it seemed, the apostle Paul wanted to go to another city to tell people about Jesus. But he spent three whole months in Ephesus "arguing and pleading" about the kingdom! Paul knew that you need considerable time to debate and argue and plead with people about such a large topic as the kingdom of God.

Gun violence, I would argue, stands deeply in opposition to everything the kingdom of God means. We need a significant amount of time to consider how to prevent it. It, too, is a large topic. Once, when I was invited to speak to a sociology class at a university in Kansas, the professor introduced me by asking the students, "If you wanted to thoroughly research the problem of gun violence in America, what academic disciplines should you consult?" The students filled the entire whiteboard with their answers: sociology, history, psychology, psychiatry, criminal justice, law, philosophy, statistics, African American studies, biblical studies, military science, political science, literature, urban studies. Those students had a sense of how wideranging the answers to the problem of gun violence really are.

They knew it to be a complicated problem, and they knew we'd need wisdom from almost every discipline to solve it.

One of my frustrations is to meet church folks who say, "Atwood, we were wondering if you'd come to our church some Sunday night and help us understand gun violence and what we can do about it. What we like to do is meet around six for a potluck, and then we'd like for you to give a thirty-minute talk on guns, followed by another twenty minutes for questions and answers. We like to end by seven thirty—and certainly no later than seven forty-five."

That's quite an order. Thirty minutes to explain a gun culture that claims forty thousand lives every year and what the church of Jesus might do about it? I'm often tempted to reply, "Sure! Then I can come again next week to cover God, humanity, and the Milky Way."

If you want people to understand why Americans are so fascinated with violence, why so many of us place our ultimate trust in firearms to protect us, and why, as a nation, we seem paralyzed to defeat a small, extremist minority of people who have never seen a gun they didn't like—well, you have to spend some time studying the matter. You can't explain the omnipresent, systemic reign of guns in a few minutes. It's one of the reasons I wrote this book.

Speaking out boldly and arguing persuasively about the kingdom of God: that's what I want to be about. When we speak boldly and argue persuasively the truth of the gospel, backed up by facts, we will save lives. We must trust the guidance of God's Spirit, which conquers our fears and gives us courage to work for the kingdom of God.

Before we can effectively work for change, we need to examine how we ended up here in the first place. Let's begin with a look at the myths about guns that circulate all around us.

2

SLOGANS WE DIE BY
Ten Myths about Guns

F IREARMS ARE SURROUNDED by a certain mystique in our culture. This mystique enables myths about guns to grow and flourish. Those myths, in turn, stimulate and perpetuate America's gun violence. These myths ignore scientific evidence. It is an ongoing heartbreak for me that our supposedly enlightened nation bases its gun policies on the mollifying myths of violence, power, and domination.

Myths are half-truths or untruths, fictions that meld together to create an ideology. *Webster's* dictionary suggests that a myth is "a notion based more on tradition or convenience than on fact."[1] President John F. Kennedy once spoke to the power of myths to lead us down these primrose paths of our own self-destruction. "The great enemy of the truth is very often not the lie—deliberate, contrived, and dishonest—but the myth—persistent, persuasive, and unrealistic," he said. "Too often we hold fast to the clichés of our forebears. We subject all facts to a prefabricated set of interpretations. We enjoy the comfort of opinion without the discomfort of thought."[2]

If the truth will set you free, as Jesus said in John 8:32, then myths will keep you bound. We simply can't build a viable, caring society on falsehoods. We need scientific research, evidence-based studies, and substantive facts. We need to look the facts straight in the eye. We need to face the reality that 82 percent of all gun deaths in the developed world occur in the United States. We need to acknowledge that 92 percent of all children and youth ages fifteen to twenty-four killed by firearms worldwide are American kids.[3] We must determine what is fact and what is fiction, what is myth and what is truth. To let myths go unchallenged only increases the collateral damage of guns that we bear every day.

In this chapter we will explore the most common and misleading myths about guns, which perpetuate obscene levels of gun violence in the United States. I hope that sooner rather than later they will be exposed to the bright light of truth. Godspeed the day!

1. Guns don't kill people; people kill people

"I hope we don't try to use this as an excuse to go and take away guns." That's what former vice president Dan Quayle said when he learned of the massacre at Columbine High School in 1999. Simple, inanimate objects that are falsely accused: for Quayle and his friends, that's what guns are. Gun rights activists urge us to concentrate on what they call the "root causes of gun violence."

They have a long list of root causes: violent movies and video games, crime programs on television, rap music, drugs, gangs, single-parent families, and lack of father figures in urban communities. The biggest root cause of all, they say, is mental illness. (We'll talk about that myth next.) No one is denying that these factors are often connected to violence. But shouldn't guns themselves qualify as at least *one* of the root causes of gun violence?

To grasp the absurdity of the slogan "Guns don't kill people; people kill people," shorten the sentence: "Guns don't kill." Really? One hundred people dead every day from guns? Tens of thousands of times, year after year, decade after decade, generation after generation, doctors and coroners have signed official papers that declare that the instrument responsible for a death was a gun. "Guns don't kill" is the most abstract, abstruse, metaphysical proposition I know of. It pushes us far beyond the supernatural and transcendent and into the land of fantasy. While the phrase "Guns don't kill people; people kill people" is ubiquitous, I've never seen it in a gun shop. Guns *do* kill: that's exactly why many people want them.

One of my friends observes, "The gun is to gun violence as the mosquito is to malaria. Break the chances of causation and the disease retreats." Saying guns don't kill people is like saying mosquitoes don't cause malaria or that influenza is not caused by a virus. Sure, there might be more going on than the mosquito or the virus. But you can't have malaria without a mosquito. You can't get the flu without a virus. And you can't have a gun death without a gun.

2. The mentally ill are the chief perpetrators of gun violence

Where should we start on this one? This myth is simply, flagrantly untrue. It is designed to take the focus off guns themselves and to place the blame on convenient scapegoats: those who struggle with mental illness. Only 4 percent of interpersonal violence in America involves the mentally ill. Such dishonest characterization by gun rights proponents that the mentally ill are the perpetrators of gun violence blocks discussion of the real risk factors for violence in the United States—low socioeconomic status, substance abuse, and a history of arrest.[4]

Every country in the world struggles with issues of mental health among its citizens, and the United States has its fair share of people who are mentally ill. But we do not have more dangerously mentally ill persons than other developed nations do. What we *do* have is twenty-five times the murder rate of other highly developed nations.[5] We can only blame that obscene reality on our easy access to guns, which other developed countries refuse to tolerate.

Yes, we must responsibly fix the flaws in our mental health system. Absolutely. But mental health concerns are *not* the major cause of gun violence. In fact, those suffering from mental illness are far more likely to be the *victims* of violence than its perpetrators.

3. When guns are outlawed, only outlaws will have guns

This particular myth is based on another myth that scares the daylights out of extremist gun lovers: namely, that there is an organized effort in America to ban all guns. No recognized political leader, or political party, or organization that works to prevent gun violence would make such a proposal. The Coalition to Stop Gun Violence, the Brady Campaign, Courage to Fight Gun Violence, Americans for Responsible Solutions: none of them are suggesting that all guns be banned. There are three reasons why believing such an effort underway is ludicrous: 1) collecting 393 million guns is unachievable; 2) millions of our citizens enjoy guns and use them responsibly, and others depend on them to feed their families or for protection from wildlife; and 3) the Second Amendment in our Constitution endorses an individual's right to own them.

Nevertheless, for many gun lovers this catchy and frightening myth is propped up by statements like "Most gunowners are good citizens and would obey any law that would restrict purchase of or access to guns. But criminals would not obey any such law. So eventually criminals would have all the guns, and the whole country would be at their mercy." Even if some mainstream gun control organization *were* proposing to take all guns out of the hands of private citizens—and again, none of them are—this myth obscures the fact that police officers and other authorities would still have guns. But myths conveniently ignore certain truths.

I'm glad the National Criminal Instant Background Check System has denied at least two million illegal gun purchases since its inauguration in 1998.[6] The question remains: Should America make it easier or harder for criminals and terrorists to get a gun? And doesn't it seem reasonable to believe that if guns are, in fact, more difficult to obtain, fewer criminals will have them?

A caveat: Since mass shootings have become so common-place in America, there is a growing movement to ban assault rifles. These are the weapons given to soldiers that are designed to kill as many people as possible within a short range. These types of firearms, if equipped with large magazines, can shoot a hundred rounds in a minute. Individual citizens do not need such overwhelming firepower. Every major Christian denomi-nation and religious body in America has called for a ban on this class of weapons. Assault weapons have no business in a civil society.

4. More guns equals less crime

This myth may sound like common sense to some people or offer comfort to those who live in fear. The idea is that hidden guns, within arm's reach of their private owners, increase pub-lic safety. Economist John Lott first developed this "more guns, less crime" theory in his 1998 book of the same title, and he has since popularized it via frequent legislative testimony and op-eds. The National Rifle Association has deployed Lott's work to beat back calls for new regulations on guns or gun ownership.

In the aftermath of the Sandy Hook Elementary School shooting in 2012, NRA leader Wayne LaPierre made his infamous assertion that "the only way to stop a bad guy with a gun is a good guy with a gun." He was tapping into an already deep-seated notion. What this argument omits is that nefarious people attack by stealth, with gun or weapon already in hand. If a potential victim reaches for a holster, purse, pocket, or shelf, he or she will most likely be shot.

This myth is a powerful and seductive untruth. It is directed particularly at Americans who favor personal liberty over communitarian ideals. It's also completely dishonest. There is no scientific study that shows that having more guns decreases crime. Scientific studies actually reveal just the opposite. A forty-year Stanford Law School study shows Lott's figures are not correct. If guns made us safer, we would be the safest country in the world. But that is not the case.[7]

5. Mass shooters attack gun-free zones knowing unarmed people cannot defend themselves

This myth is a form of blaming victims for their own deaths. It effectively suggests that innocent people praying in houses of worship or studying in a college library or teaching in a school are to blame for their own deaths because they were not armed.[8]

The NRA and President Donald Trump promote this kind of disinformation. But as the *Washington Post* reports, researchers have discovered that:

> The overwhelming majority of people who commit mass public shootings are suicidal at the time of their attacks: They

fully intend to die, either by a self-inflicted gunshot wound or a shootout with police. . . . Nearly half the perpetrators of mass shootings carried out between 1982 and 2018 took their own lives at or near the scene of their crime, according to a mass shooting database maintained by *Mother Jones* magazine. [If we include] individuals who were shot and killed during subsequent encounters with police, . . . about 7 in 10 mass shooters don't survive. Certainty of death, in other words, is no deterrent to mass shooters. Most of them may, in fact, be driven by it.[9]

6. An armed society is a polite society

With 393 million guns in the United States—enough for every man, woman, and child, with hundreds of thousands left over—we are the most heavily armed country in the free world. In 2016, an additional 16 million guns came off our assembly lines or were imported. If this myth were true— that an armed society is a polite society—then we should *already* be the most polite people on the face of the earth. Have you noticed any uptick in American courtesy and politeness lately? I haven't.

Some people optimistically quote some obscure data and shout that robust gun sales have driven down crime rates and murder rates. That small decline may, in fact, be welcome news. What is *not* welcome are the statistics which show that, in the last few years, the number of Americans who are shot each year is going up. This includes both fatal and nonfatal shootings, murders, assaults, suicides and suicide attempts, accidents, and police shootings. In the year 2010 alone, according to data compiled by the Giffords Law Center, 104,581 people were killed or injured by firearms. That's 31,076 homicides, suicides, and unintentional shootings; 73,505 persons were treated in hospital emergency departments for gunshot wounds.[10] Nor can we forget that more than 219,000 students have experienced gun violence at their schools since Columbine. Since 1999, there have been an average of ten school shootings each year in the United States.[11]

7. If it weren't a gun, it would have been a baseball bat

I cannot count how many times I have heard this myth. People who recite this myth do so to defend gun ownership. They suggest it doesn't really matter what weapon people have access to: people intent on violence will carry it out, and we should not blame guns—"The poor, inanimate things that they are"—for America's violence.

But if someone is murderously enraged and the only weapon at that person's disposal is a baseball bat, the victim might end up with a concussion or a broken arm—assuming that the assailant can first of all chase down the other person. On the other hand, if someone is furious and carries around a handgun, the outcome is most likely to be deadly.

I've never heard of a drive-by knifing. Have you? Many instruments can indeed be deadly, but they are not in and of themselves considered violent tools, and therefore are relatively inefficient devices in the hands of someone who seeks to harm another. Handguns are *by far* the most frequently used murder weapon in the United States. In 2017, 7,032 people were murdered with handguns. Knives or cutting instruments were the second most widely used weapons, with 1,591 murders committed with a knife. These are followed by blunt instruments and personal weapons (such as hands and feet), rifles, shotguns, narcotics, and fire.[12] For decades, those in America who are determined to maim and kill have chosen guns. Why? They are the most efficient.

8. Guns save lives

This myth contends that the very presence of a firearm, without a shot being fired, somehow prevents crime. To support this myth, the National Rifle Association uses bulked-up numbers that come from one of their favorite researchers, Gary Kleck. Kleck claims in the *American Rifleman*, the mouthpiece of the NRA, that "6,850 times a day, every 13 seconds, law-abiding people use their guns to defend themselves and their families against criminals, or 2.5 million times a year."[13]

Research done by established epidemiologists encourage us to reject Kleck's work, and for several reasons. The major one is that Kleck's numbers are, simply put, *mathematically impossible*. Reliable data from hospital records, national crime victimization surveys, gun violence archives, and police records indicate that his numbers are completely wrong.[14]

You could argue that guns *can* save some lives. But the reality is that guns *take* many more lives, and at incredible rates. As noted earlier, research shows that a gun kept in the home for self-defense is twelve times more likely to be used in an accidental shooting or death of a family member or other household member than to stop an intruder.[15]

Put simply, no reputable scientific study shows that having a gun for self-defense increases security.

9. Gun control does not work

This myth suggests that gun control legislation is ineffective. Advocates for this myth are quick to say, "Take a look at Chicago!" Or they point to other large cities, like Washington, D.C., which have strong gun laws but suffer high murder and crime rates. If robust gun legislation in places like Chicago isn't reducing gun violence, they argue, then gun control must not work.

But like all myths, that's much too simplistic. One of the most wonderful features of living in the United States is that we can freely travel from one city or state to another. But when it comes to the free flow of guns, a gunrunner's easy mobility constitutes a huge problem. Many jurisdictions with strong gun laws are bordered by jurisdictions with weak laws. Such is the case for Chicago and Washington, D.C., where geography helps explain and promote their dilemma.

Let's focus on Chicago. Yes, the city has very strong gun laws, but the state of Illinois has very weak ones. Those who want a gun can take a short drive just beyond Chicago's city limits to find a friendly gun dealer. Illinois exports crime guns at a rate that is less than half the national average, but it has the second highest crime gun *import* rate.[16]

Another option for Chicagoans is to drive a few miles south to Indiana, where gun laws are even weaker and people from all over can do one-stop gun shopping for most any kind of firearm they might want. For example, Indiana does not

- prohibit the transfer or possession of assault weapons, .50-caliber rifles, or large capacity ammunition magazines;
- require a background check before the transfer of a firearm between private parties;
- license firearm owners;
- require the registration of firearms;
- limit the number of firearms that may be purchased at one time;
- impose a waiting period on firearm purchases; or
- regulate unsafe handguns.[17]

So if one is eager to get a gun, Indiana is just thirty minutes away from Chicago.

10. Calling an AR-15 or AK-47 an "assault weapon" is misleading

"Eschew Obfuscation." Have you seen this bumper sticker? You can bet your house it was not on the car of a gun aficionado. The linguistic war over what to label certain guns illustrates how the gun industry and its supporters obfuscate reality and try to control damage to their image. In *Making a Killing: The Business of Guns in America*, Tom Diaz writes, "The question of what to call this awkward class of firearms has become increasingly important in the debate over efforts to control them."[18]

People who argue on behalf of this myth say that AR-15s and AK-47s are simply semiautomatic guns—no different from the semiautomatic rifles that have been in common use for almost one hundred years and that typically use significantly less powerful cartridges. They say that to malign anything because you think it looks scary is silly.

But the term *assault weapon* was actually created by the gun industry itself, not gun violence prevention advocates. It goes all the way back to the 1980s, when gun aficionados, together with the "urban survivalist movement" they represented, wanted more modern military look-alike guns.[19] So why is the corporate gun lobby retreating from calling this class of firearms "assault weapons," as the lobby itself labeled them in the early 1980s? Perhaps it is because these weapons have become the undeniable choice of mass shooters and the public wants them banned. No matter what you call it, *any* gun that can shoot a hundred bullets in less than one minute has no place on the streets of America.

Where did the myths come from?

We all fall prey to myths at points in our lives. We all become convinced by slogans and half-truths. But the myths we have just looked at are more than an innocent blurring of the truth. They have become death-dealing lies—slogans Americans die by. If these myths continue to hold such sway that policies and laws stay the same, one need not be clairvoyant to know there will be yet more shootings, more muggings, more murders, suicides, and accidents. We will continue to bury forty thousand people a year. Collateral damage will continue to accrue.

These myths didn't just appear out of thin air. Let's turn now to look at where these myths come from—who benefits from them, how they circulate, and where they began. How did we as citizens get hoodwinked into believing that these gun myths are gospel truth?

3

"IN THIS GAME FOR KEEPS"
A Short History of Gundamentalism

G UN VIOLENCE HAS not always plagued the United States
the way it does today. In days past, our citizens would
not stand for it. Even the idea that the "Wild West" was rife
with gun violence is more myth than truth. Yes, Tombstone,
Arizona, today advertises "Gunfights Daily," and tourists line
up each afternoon to watch costumed cowboys and lawmen
reenact the bloody gunfight at the O.K. Corral with blazing six-
guns. But as with much of the Wild West, myth has replaced
history. The actual 1881 shootout took place in a narrow alley,
not at the corral. In fact, the American West's most infamous
gun battle erupted when the marshal tried to enforce a local
ordinance that barred carrying firearms in public. Law scholar
Adam Winkler writes, "Frontier towns handled guns the way a
Boston restaurant today handles overcoats in the winter. New
arrivals were required to turn in their guns to authorities in exchange for something like a metal token."[1] I recently saw an old
picture of Main Street in Dodge City with a huge sign that read
"The Carrying of Firearms Strictly Prohibited."

Even the National Rifle Association, founded in 1871 by a former reporter for the *New York Times*, used to support extensive gun control laws. You read that right: the NRA used to support gun control! When concealed carry of weapons was so popular in the 1920s and 1930s, some leaders of the NRA drafted legislation for waiting periods for handgun buyers. They also championed the 1934 and 1938 National Firearms Acts that created a licensing system for gun dealers. The NRA also favored almost all prohibitive taxes on owning a machine gun.[2]

After President Kennedy was shot in 1963, Franklin Orth, president of the NRA, testified before Congress that mail-ordering of shotguns and rifles should not be allowed.[3] (Incidentally, such a law would have prohibited my first gun purchase, from a Sears catalog.)

So when did things change? In 1977 at their annual convention in Cincinnati, the NRA spun 180 degrees. They thumbed their noses at their former gun safety programs, training law enforcement, and mentoring Boy Scouts on marksmanship and the safe handling of guns. Instead they followed the money and supplied frightened citizens with handguns. Under the leadership of Harlan Carter and Neal Knox, NRA members pulled a successful coup d'état and threw out the old guard leadership for their new hard line that Americans should never be separated from their guns.[4] That was when the NRA gained its reputation as the invincible "gun lobby" and adopted policies to stop any effort to modify, restrict, or regulate the sale of any gun to anybody for any reason. Their new doctrine was ultimately rooted in the fear that "all gun-control laws lead inexorably to the complete confiscation of all firearms."[5] That policy is today the NRA's North Star by which they steer their organization.

The day he was installed as executive vice president of the NRA, Harlan Carter announced: "Beginning in this place and at this hour, this period in NRA history is finished." Up until then the NRA had focused on things like hunting clinics, courses on hunting safety, target shooting, and marksmanship contests. From this point on, writes Osha Gray Davidson in *Under Fire: The NRA and the Battle for Gun Control*, "the new NRA would be devoted single-mindedly—and proud of the fact—to the proposition that Americans and their guns must never, *never* be parted." As Carter later testified before Congress, "We are in this game for keeps."[6]

What is gundamentalism?

Since then, the NRA has been true to Carter's vision. The group has fought every single gun regulation to come before individual states and the U.S. Congress. The corporate gun lobby, made up of firearm and ammunition manufacturers, the NRA, and other gun rights groups, influences public policy and law to such an extent that legislation today protects guns rather than people.

We can call this *gundamentalism*: a religious devotion to guns that shapes people's perspectives to such an extent that their worldview, affections, and identity gather around the purchase, maintenance, carrying, and shooting of as many guns as possible. Gundamentalists believe, wholeheartedly, the myths we looked at in chapter 2. Gundamentalism is such a force in American society today that I wrote an entire book about it: *Gundamentalism and Where It Is Taking America.*

Gundamentalists, then, are those who 1) go beyond the language of the Second Amendment and understand the right to "keep and bear arms" as a tenet of religious or quasi-religious faith; 2) believe one's understanding of the Second Amendment gives one additional rights to harass, slander, defame, and stalk those who believe otherwise; and 3) remain willfully ignorant and unwilling to accept differing views of the Second Amendment that come through scientific gun studies and court rulings.[7]

It's important to note here that only a tiny fraction of gun owners can legitimately be called gundamentalists. Today's gun owners, for the most part, differ widely from their elite leaders who command seven-figure salaries from the imposing NRA headquarters in Fairfax County, Virginia.[8] At an event eight days after the 2018 Parkland high school shooting in Florida, Wisconsin senator Tammy Baldwin said, "We know that we need change. And it's frustrating, because there is a high level of consensus across America on the sort of common-sense safety measures that need to be brought up and passed. Among gun owners—and I'm a gun owner myself—97 percent of us support expanded, universal background checks so we don't have the gun show loophole, so that we don't have the Internet purchases that don't go through a thorough background check."

Did you get that? Baldwin's claim, which PolitiFact Wisconsin labeled "mostly on target," is that the *vast majority* of gun owners—97 percent—support requiring background checks for all gun sales, not just those done by federally licensed dealers.[9]

So not all gun owners are gundamentalists. But this sliver of gun-loving extremists holds the rest of the country hostage, not only with their out-of-touch views but with their deeply troubling social behavior. And most of our gun legislation caters to these gundamentalists rather than protecting the public's safety. Their power incarnates the phrase "The squeaky wheel gets the grease."

How gundamentalism protects guns

For hundreds of years, our nation lived comfortably with both gun rights and "gun control" measures. In fact, the Constitution requires it. The Second Amendment both guarantees the right to keep and bear arms *and* offers assurance that such arms be "well regulated." The Second Amendment is the only constitutional right that is accompanied by a regulation. The amendment reads (emphasis mine), "*A well regulated Militia*, being necessary to the security of a free State, the right of the people to keep and bear Arms, shall not be infringed."

Consider that full sentence for a minute. The Second Amendment is not simply a right for those who choose to own guns; it equally assures a collective right for every American to know that instruments which are made to kill are, in fact, *well regulated*. This is not a radical idea. It is in full accord with the U.S. Constitution. The Second Amendment belongs to all Americans. It does not exist for the sole benefit of those who love guns or who choose to arm themselves. It belongs to us all.

Yet our gun laws are a hodgepodge of regulations designed to protect the selling of all firearms and to make it doubly difficult for law enforcement to disrupt any sales. Gundamentalism operates at all levels.

If guns were actually "well regulated," as the Constitution stipulates, the United States would not be fraught with so much danger and death. But firearms are not anywhere close to being well regulated. In fact, there are millions of cheap guns out there in people's closets, bedside stands, and attics that were manufactured without built-in safeties. Millions more were made with such inferior steel they are not accurate beyond nostril range. If dropped from a table, they would most likely fire. These guns are not called "junk guns" for no reason. Any sensible gun owner would never own one.

Yet laws protect even these substandard weapons. The U.S. Consumer Products Safety Act of 1972 prohibits the Consumer Protection Agency or any other government agency from examining the safety of any gun or any piece of ammunition. Toy rabbits, teddy bears, and toy guns have four sets of laws to protect our infants and toddlers from harm: loose parts, rough edges, flammability, and toxicity. But government regulations on real guns, even for safety reasons, are forbidden.

Before the election of President George W. Bush, the NRA boasted that if he won, they would have an office in the White House. They were right. Just consider that tragic meeting in 2005 when President Bush signed into law the Protection of Lawful Commerce in Arms Act. This legislation makes it difficult for citizens to press charges against gun manufacturers or dealers for unnecessary deaths. The law denies victims of gun violence the right to sue those involved in the manufacture, distribution, or sale of guns for improper or negligent conduct.[10] No other industry enjoys such immunity. Gundamentalists wield enormous power.

Gundamentalism is also at the root of Congress's inability to pass common-sense gun laws in the wake of mass shootings. In her provocative article "This Cruel Parody of Representation," novelist Marilynne Robinson claims that Republican lawmakers have acted decisively on our country's urgent problems by not acting at all. The reasons for their inaction, she says, related to money and the inertia it brings, stymie the possibilities of profound social change. To illuminate her thesis, Robinson takes on gun violence:

> Whenever some new massacre is perpetrated in this country, the usual voices say that the tragedy should not be politicized. This response is so inevitable that it can be assumed to produce the desired effect: the tamping down of outrage in deference to the horror of the crime. Their right to sanctimoniousness having been tacitly conceded, these concerned voices add that in such moments of national crisis, we must all come together as we keep

the slaughtered and their families in our thoughts and prayers. There should be no divisiveness, they say, which in practical terms means no assigning of responsibility. . . . [T]he public is hushed like children, closed out of the deliberations of an inner circle who knowingly weigh their own interests against the certainty that Americans will again die en masse in their schools, theaters, and churches. Thoughts and prayers cost nothing, and they offend no donors.[11]

And gundamentalism is the taproot of legislation such as "stand your ground" laws, which enable people to shoot first and think later. Here is one example:

> Britany Jacobs and two of her children were waiting in a car for her boyfriend, Markeis McGlockton, and their 5-year-old son to return from a snack run. . . . Michael Drejka approached the car and began to berate Ms. Jacobs for parking in a handicapped space. Hearing the commotion, Mr. McGlockton emerged from the store and shoved Mr. Drejka to the ground. He had just taken a step away when Mr. Drejka pulled out a gun and shot him in the chest. Mr. McGlockton then ran into the convenience store, where he bled to death as his five-year-old son stood screaming beside him.[12]

Surveillance footage from the Florida convenience store clearly shows that Drejka fired the shot that killed McGlockton. Even so, a day after the shooting, the county sheriff said that Drejka would not be arrested. The sheriff cited Florida's "stand your ground" law, which says that anyone who "reasonably believes" that deadly force is necessary "to prevent imminent death or great bodily harm" does not have a duty to retreat. Similar laws exist in over two dozen states. As the *Washington Post* editorial board observed, "By creating a more lax standard for the use of lethal force, the laws excuse and perhaps incentivize reckless violence." Furthermore, the *Post* noted, the laws are exacerbated by racial bias. "It may not just be a coincidence in this case," they wrote, "that the shooter is white and the victim African American."[13] As we will see more clearly soon, gundamentalism is not racially neutral.

How gundamentalism shapes all of us

Gundamentalism can flavor conversations about gun violence in unexpected ways. It stands behind the resignation all of us begin to feel when shootings become a normal part of daily life. The 158th mass shooting in the United States in 2018 occurred at the *Capital Gazette* newspaper offices in Annapolis, Maryland, on June 28. Five people were slaughtered. I was dumbstruck by the reporter who tried to put a positive spin on the tragedy by praising the amazing speed at which law enforcement arrived at the scene. They arrived within ninety seconds (some said sixty seconds). Under duress, the officers synchronized their communication equipment and within two minutes entered the building to confront the gunman.[14] As the reporter noted, "Twenty years ago, we were so unaccustomed to mass shootings that it took us a long time to secure an area and get things under control. We had to figure out who was to do what. Today, law enforcement was at the scene in ninety seconds. Each knew their protocols and could begin immediately to work together."

While I'm grateful for the bravery and professionalism of first responders in getting to the *Capital Gazette* offices so quickly, it sickens me to realize we are today *so accustomed to mass shootings* that law enforcement today is particularly skilled in responding to and confronting such situations. Praising the work of first responders: Is that the best we can do in dealing with such catastrophes? Why is it taking us so long to get our social and legislative protocols in order so we can avoid the calamity of mass shootings altogether? Just a few simple gun laws would dramatically prevent many gun deaths while depriving no one of their Second Amendment rights. It is indeed noteworthy for law enforcement to reach crime scenes quickly and with protocols all in order, but it is small comfort to realize we are so accustomed to mass shootings that we now know "just what to do" in such a needless disaster.

The real question is, Why have we grown so *accustomed* to war scenes in our places of business, schools, and houses of worship? Why don't we put more effort into stopping mass shootings in the first place? Why has every other developed country in the world managed to all but eliminate mass shootings? Why don't we? When New Zealand suffered a horrible mass shooting at two mosques in Christchurch in 2019, it took them six days to write legislation that banned all semiautomatic weapons and large magazines. Imagine. Why are we so paralyzed?

Gundamentalism—an extreme affection for and even worship of guns—might have something to do with it.

Gundamentalism and whiteness

We cannot talk about gundamentalism without talking about racism and domination, which we will explore more in chapter 8. Native Americans were the first peoples on these shores to experience the cruel domination of white Europeans. Through colonization and slavery, the United States of America created and embraced a system of valuing and devaluing people according to skin color and ethnic identity. The name for this system is white supremacy. This system has deliberately subjugated Indigenous peoples, African Americans, Asian Americans, Latinos, and others for the material, political, and social advantage of white people. The continuing legacy of white supremacy is visible in large and small ways.

The hate-filled militia movement and white nationalism are manifestations of white supremacy, whose advocates boast about their weaponry. In fact, no hate group can survive without depending on violence and firearms. The collateral damage of gundamentalism and white supremacy can be seen in the rise of hate crimes throughout the country. As the violence in Charlottesville, Virginia, in August 2017 demonstrated, neo-Nazis and white supremacist militias have been emboldened to spew their message of hate toward Jews and people of color, in large part because the U.S. president has refused to criticize their rhetoric, tactics, or ideology. Shortly after the deadly white nationalist rally, President Trump equated the philosophies of white supremacists with that of their antiracist protesters. "There are good people on both sides," he said.

The Southern Poverty Law Center (SPLC), a legal advocacy organization that tracks hate groups, reports that hate and domestic extremism are rising "in an unabated trend." As reported on NPR, "the center found a 30 percent increase in U.S. hate groups over the past four years and a 7 percent increase in hate groups in 2018 alone." It designated 1,020 organizations as hate groups in 2018, the highest number in at least twenty years. Most of these organizations are driven by white supremacist ideology. The most visible groups are neo-Nazis, the Ku Klux Klan, white nationalists, racist skinheads, and neo-Confederates. The SPLC reports that in reaction to the flourishing of white supremacists, Black nationalist groups are also growing. These groups are "often anti-Semitic, anti-LGBT and anti-white but, unlike white nationalist groups, [they] have little support and basically no sway in politics."[15]

Of the more than 7,100 hate crimes reported last year, nearly three in five were motivated by race or ethnicity. Religion and sexual orientation were the other two primary motivators.[16]

Hate and the desire to dominate others come from a heretical and total misunderstanding of power we find described in Genesis 1. The text declares that God created man and woman in God's image and instructed them to be fruitful and multiply. God says, "Fill the earth and subdue it; and have dominion over the fish of the sea and over the birds of the air and over every living thing that moves upon the earth" (Genesis 1:28).

God gave humankind dominion over the animals, but God did not give any nation, or any person, or any group of persons—however powerful, however rich—dominion over other human beings. The Hebrew word for dominion is *radah*; it means "to reign" or "to rule over." But we must be very careful with this word. The verse in which it appears is one of the most misinterpreted and deliberately misconstrued verses in all the Bible.

The theologian Walter Brueggemann reminds us that the biblical understanding of dominion is similar to the work of a gentle shepherd who knows each of his flock by name and leads them into green pastures and beside still waters. If danger comes, the shepherd lays down his life for the sheep. *That* is the kind of dominion the Almighty expects God's people to exhibit before the world. In transferring our behaviors to the political scene, the word *dominion* refers to those practical deeds of love offered to the mental, physical, and spiritual welfare of all of God's people, who are loved equally by their Creator.[17]

We have seen in the preceding paragraphs how the dominion God gave humankind has historically been corrupted to legitimize white supremacy. It perpetuates the ideas that might makes right and that those with the gold and the guns make all the rules. With this self-seeking and deliberate misuse of Holy Scripture comes the cruel and domineering behavior we find in both racism and gundamentalism.

Peter Marty, publisher of *Christian Century*, cites the wisdom of C. S. Lewis's *Screwtape Letters*: hatred is "often the *compensation* by which a frightened man reimburses himself for the miseries of Fear. The more he fears, the more he will hate."[18] Marty concludes, "Plotting the misery index of fear in our individual lives and communities explains why so many scared people are busily reimbursing themselves with hate. But people of deep faith don't play that reimbursement game. They are focused on wearing down hate-filled souls through beautiful acts of love."[19] As noted earlier, we will look more closely at the intersection of gundamentalism and racism in chapter 8.

What gundamentalism sows

So why do we allow anyone to easily get a gun? Why do we place so few regulations on killing machines? Research reveals that the most gun deaths occur where the most guns are. That is not a coincidence. The math cannot be denied.

Table 1. *States ranked according to highest and lowest gun death rates*

Rank	State	Household gun ownership (%)	Gun deaths per 100,000
		Five highest	
1	Alaska	56.4	23.86
2	Alabama	49.5	21.51
3	Louisiana	49.0	21.08
4	Mississippi	54.3	19.64
5	Oklahoma	46.7	19.52
		Five lowest	
46	Connecticut	22.2	4.81
47	Rhode Island	15.9	4.64
48	Hawaii	12.5	4.62
49	New York	22.2	4.56
50	Massachusetts	14.3	3.55

Source: Centers for Disease Control and Prevention, National Center for Injury Prevention and Control via the Gun Violence Archive.

In 2016, Alaska had the highest per capita gun death rate, followed by Alabama (see table 1). As the Violence Policy Center notes, "Each of these states has extremely lax gun laws as well as a higher rate of gun ownership." Meanwhile, Massachusetts and New York, the states with the lowest gun death rates in the nation, have "strong gun violence prevention laws and a lower rate of gun ownership."[20] When guns are readily available, they are used.

Not only are more people dying by guns; more people are being shot.[21] Thankfully, not all those who are shot die, but one does not easily recover from the trauma of being a target, much less being hit. Being shot, or even being shot at, does something to the psyche. Guns pose such a huge risk that simply having one pointed in your direction causes psychological distress even years later. The authors of one observational study write that "firearm victimization is associated with increased levels of distress, greater than the effects of the victimization itself. These findings may be explained by the fear of death being increased in situations involving more lethal weapons."[22] For an existential portrayal of this reality, see the page 25 account of the trauma experienced by the daughter of one of my colleagues who was mugged at the barrel of a gun and had her car stolen. Years later she is haunted by that memory.

When people witness a traumatic and violent event, they experience shock and can struggle to feel safe again. People who only hear about or see coverage of the event can also struggle to feel safe in their community. As one therapy provider notes, "The effects of gun violence are widespread and impact those in the community as well as people all across the country."[23]

With 393 million guns in the nation, sooner or later, vast numbers of them will be used for the purpose for which they were made. There is no need to sugarcoat that truth. Guns are made to kill.

To our shame, we have deliberately chosen not to do anything to keep thousands of our neighbors alive. Such callousness is not a sign of a great country. It is a sign of a country that is cold-hearted and looks especially ridiculous compared with other countries in the world. If we had no choice about protecting those who are destined to die at the barrels of a gun, or if no alternatives were available to keep people alive, we would simply accept their deaths as we accept the deaths of those killed by hurricanes, earthquakes, and natural disasters. Barring certain interventions, like earthquake-resilient architecture, the deaths that occur in a natural disaster are accepted as being beyond our control. But we *are* capable of preventing thousands of gun deaths by putting in place a few simple measures that would protect lives. We can do this without threatening Second Amendment rights. When guns are "well regulated," as the Constitution stipulates, criminals will have much less opportunity to acquire them.

Hope beyond gundamentalism

The inability or reluctance of our faith communities to address gun violence as a moral, ethical, and spiritual problem, coupled with our elected leaders' fears of a tiny but powerful minority of gundamentalists, has resulted in laws that exacerbate crime instead of curtailing it, weaken law enforcement instead of strengthening it, and make it easier for terrorists, domestic abusers, and other dangerous individuals to get weapons. For example, instead of freeing governmental regulatory agencies to limit individuals on the FBI's suspected terrorist list or the Transportation Security Administration's "no fly" list from buying firearms and explosives, the corporate gun lobby writes legislation that enables such individuals to continue buying guns and explosives.[24]

Just imagine the effect of one simple regulation that requires an instantaneous background check on all guns sold in America! More than 90 percent of the American people favor such a law, including gun owners and even members of the NRA. If that provision were enacted into law, there would be a precipitous drop in the number of people killed and assaulted by guns.

Let me reiterate something I said at the beginning of the chapter: Most gun owners are not gundamentalists. The gun owners I know are polite and civic minded and belong to a growing movement that supports sensible gun reform. We are searching to find some middle ground so we can build the America we all want. The progress is slow, but it is sure. We await the arrival of more good citizens and strong, rational voices from the silent majority of gun owners who are willing to take a risk for love's sake.

Surely the days are coming when our legislators will grow less beholden to the NRA and the corporate gun lobby and we will have common-sense gun laws. I'm betting my life on it. God promises us a day when, as Isaiah 11:9 says, "they shall not hurt or destroy in all my holy mountain; for the earth shall be full of the knowledge of the Lord as the waters cover the sea."

4

FEAR AND INCIVILITY
Living in a Nation with More Guns Than People

LIVE IN WHAT is often called "gun country." Just a few miles away from my home in Harrisonburg, Virginia, a young man was arrested in 2018 for shooting a handgun into a moving vehicle driven by someone he did not know. Further charges were added for altering the weapon's serial number.[1] Was he drunk, or was he just "out having fun"? Did he want to see a wreck, or did he want to kill somebody? Does it matter?

Two months after this incident, the local police department charged another man for a similar crime. This man was charged with felonies for shooting from a vehicle, shooting at an occupied vehicle, and distributing marijuana, as well as charged with misdemeanors for brandishing a firearm and reckless handling of a firearm.[2]

When these incidents happened, I quickly dismissed them and similar outrageous events from my mind. I'm not alone in my very short memory when it comes to gun violence. Such easy dismissal of gun misuse is rampant in America. It is so ugly a subject we cannot keep it in our minds for long. When we hear of such reckless stupidity and meanness with guns, we are outraged for a day or two, but then we quickly forget it as we move on to other more pressing or pleasing concerns.

As gun violence festers in the world around us, we lose our sense of outrage and our ability to feel appalled. We become so numb to the absurdity of it all that nothing surprises us anymore.

Rudeness and incivility

I'm not alone in thinking that in the last decade the American people have grown increasingly impolite. I could be wrong, but I think bad manners took root across the nation as we watched leaders of both political parties try to elevate their own political clout and overt partisanship at the expense of the well-being of the nation. As a result, we are governed today by slogans, myths, and misinformation that fit our personal narratives, and too many of us are afraid to look at the plain, unvarnished truth. John 8:32 says that the truth will set us free, but in a rude society, truth is fragile and elusive, particularly when people start citing so-called alternative facts. In August 2018, Rudy Giuliani, President Trump's lawyer, wasn't kidding when he declared, "Truth isn't truth."[3] What a change from the words of the late senator Daniel Patrick Moynihan, who liked to say, "Everyone is entitled to their own opinion, but not to their own facts."[4]

Today, it seems that truth is defined by where one sits and what television station is on. And when people don't agree with someone's particular narrative, guns can be great intimidators. They play a huge role in the subversion of the truth and an accompanying decline of civility that pits neighbor against neighbor, race against race, religion against religion, and political party against political party. For decades, the U.S. Congress has endorsed an unexamined "gun rights" platform. They have declared that easily accessible firearms are more essential to the nation's health and well-being than keeping our citizens safe from being shot.

Naturally, the American people are nervous about that. I remember a day when we didn't hesitate to honk a horn at a reckless driver on the highway or to alert the person ahead of us who didn't step on the gas shortly after the light turned green. But not now. With men and women packing concealed weapons, many of us hesitate to honk after the light changes, because we know the other driver may have a gun. One of my parishioners was threatened at gunpoint for honking at a driver in the parking lot of an upscale shopping center near Arlington, Virginia.

I remember the day when office managers were not anxious about terminating the employment of a totally incompetent employee. Today, it gives them pause; they are aware that disgruntled former employees all over the country have "gone postal" and returned to their old offices and blown away entire staffs. It's happened frequently enough to be etched in employers' minds.

There is a growing awareness in our country that when guns are present, there is a good chance they will be used. They kill and maim; and as more violence occurs, fear increases, and people buy more guns for protection, only expanding the vicious circle.

We seldom hear about the preamble to the Constitution of the United States. It is only one sentence long, but what a sentence! The purpose of the preamble, like every other preamble, is to introduce the reasons a document needed to be written in the first place. The raison d'être for the Constitution of the

United States is succinctly spelled out in the preamble's fifty-two words. To refresh our memories, here it is (emphasis mine):

> We the People of the United States, in Order to form a more perfect Union, establish Justice, *insure domestic Tranquility*, provide for the common defence, promote the general Welfare, and secure the Blessings of Liberty to ourselves and our Posterity, do ordain and establish this Constitution for the United States of America.

All seven articles and twenty-seven amendments that follow are in response to the preamble. Yet the NRA's Wayne LaPierre, along with gundamentalists everywhere, contends that the most important part of our Constitution is the Second Amendment. LaPierre and other gundamentalists seem to forget both the "well regulated" phrase in that amendment and the promise of domestic tranquility in the preamble. "The guys with the guns make the rules," LaPierre has said. "Freedom always rides with a firearm by its side."[5]

I know of no more destructive proclamation for our democracy than those words. What is depressing and harmful to America is this confrontational language that puts the whole country on edge while rudeness and incivility spread like a cancer. Worst of all, gun extremists are seldom, if ever, confronted by our highest elected officials.

The imaginary glamour of armed vigilante action that throws down the gauntlet before police and governmental authority has no place in our democratic society. One of my friends says, "The whole point of deciding issues by the ballot box is to keep our disagreements from devolving into this armed confrontation." An all-or-nothing approach to gun regulation, which rejects any and all common-sense middle-ground positions, is uncivil and un-American.

In their book *Guns, Democracy, and the Insurrectionist Idea*, Casey Anderson and Joshua Horwitz write, "What makes the Insurrectionist propaganda so insidious is not just its effect on gun policy but also its role in advancing an antigovernment ideology that is hostile to progressive values and democratic institutions. The ideology behind the gun rights movement rejects community and consensus building in favor of a social compact that may be dissolved at any time, by anyone, on the basis of one's narrow conceptions of self-interest. In this view, might (whether political or physical) makes right, and government can never make legitimate claims against individuals on behalf of the community, even when decisions are made by democratic means with strong guarantees for individual rights."[6]

Rudeness is part of the collateral damage that emanates from this social trust in guns. Incivility is connected to the hundreds of millions of guns that are stashed away in our bedside stands, closets, and purses and concealed on our own bodies.

Language

Even our language and emotions are among the countless intangible casualties of collateral damage. Language is profoundly shaped by guns and our gun culture. Even those of us who work against gun violence sometimes find ourselves using gun-saturated phrases such as "go down to the third bullet on the page" and "shoot me an email" and "I'm under the gun" to get a project completed.

Those may seem like relatively inconsequential metaphors, but words matter. I read of a little boy who found some flowers in a wastebasket. He asked his mother why they were there. She answered, "Because they are dead. I threw them out." He replied, "Well, who shot them?"

Fearful children

America's children are afraid. And why wouldn't they be? The actual chance that a child will be killed in a school shooting is not high: one in two million. Those odds do not signal imminent danger, but millions of our kids still *feel* endangered. They do not need an actual shooting or attack to be terrified. The reporting of every mass shooting for days on end puts children in the midst of what they feel is a never-ending crime scene.[7] The youngest of our children do not understand time sequence, and many of them think that the news in America is about one shooting after another and that they could be next.

We'll look more at the issue of guns in schools in later chapters. But every day, gun threats send classrooms across the United States into active-shooter drills or lockdown modes. Children are frightened by these drills even when adults tell them it's "just practice." During active-shooter drills, kids as young as four are required to hide in darkened closets and bathrooms. To assume that these preparatory scenarios don't have a lasting effect on impressionable children is, well, wrong.

In some cities, children don't want to go to the local playground, because that is where kids get shot. Just as lead in the pipes and water supply of Flint, Michigan, has had devastating, long-term physical and psychological effects on its citizens, so the overwhelming presence of so many guns, and the violent atmosphere they spawn, has long-term, injurious effect on the minds and psyches of our children.

I recently had a conversation with Waltrina Barnett, a teacher in Wilmington, North Carolina. She told me of a third-grade boy who came to her office one morning while his class was taking a test. He sat down and began to cry. He told his teacher he had heard gunshots in the night but had managed to go back to sleep. In the morning, he learned the gunshots had been directed at his uncle, who was killed. How can anyone, let alone an eight-year-old child, put a family member's murder on his mental back burner so he can take a test? Barnett lamented the day-to-day realities of her classrooms. She said that whenever there is a shooting in North Wilmington, many neighborhood children come to class the next day depressed or angry.

Should we be surprised? Should the citizens of Wilmington "just get over it" and accept this psychic damage as a new norm? Should we put more guns in the hands of more men, women, and children to stop the gun violence? Or should we put our best minds to work so we can stop the carnage?

Thankfully, there are those who work tirelessly to seek the welfare of the city as the prophet counseled in Jeremiah 29:7. New Hanover County, North Carolina, is launching a resiliency task force to respond to the trauma of adverse childhood experiences (ACEs) in children's lives. Studies show that ACEs affect the brains of children and youth who experience trauma or witness violence regularly. They are at much greater risk for a variety of mental health issues: depression and suicide attempts, poor academic performance, alcoholism, substance abuse, sexually transmitted infections, delinquency, and violent behavior. But not only do these ACEs make the present problematic; the studies show these youth are at least two times more likely to suffer heart attacks and strokes in the future. These costs weigh especially heavily on the shoulders of young Black Americans and make it very difficult for them to escape the clutches of poverty, racism, and violence. I have a stake in this promising program in part because my daughter Mebane Boyd is chairing this task force of civic-minded educators, medical and health professionals, law enforcement, lawyers, and judges to present a unified plan for the county to become a resilient, thriving community.[8]

For years, sociologist Patrick Sharkey has been studying the persistence of racial and economic inequality in urban areas and the part that violence plays in making and keeping people poor. His studies indicate that nearly three in four Black families who live in poor, segregated neighborhoods live in the same neighborhoods and economic conditions that they did in the 1970s. The conditions affect consecutive generations. Sharkey writes, "A half-century of public policy has served to reinforce the walls of the ghetto while systematically divesting in black urban communities."[9]

The juxtaposition of two pieces of mail that arrived at my house on a blistering hot July day got my attention. One was the joyful front cover of the *New Yorker* that pictured a jubilant crowd of children and youth being showered by a water hydrant spewing cool water on them. Everyone is smiling, laughing, and giggling. In urban America, one of childhood's simple pleasures in the hot summer is to play around water hydrants and get soaked to the bone with cool, refreshing water. In the Big Apple, those moments are free. That picture brought me joy.

I was soon brought low by a second piece of mail: The *Washington Post* carried a front-page article about ten-year-old Makiyah Wilson. She had recently celebrated her birthday and was excited to start fifth grade. Wanting to cool off on a hot summer night, Makiyah was heading to an ice cream truck near her home in Northeast D.C. But then masked men drove up and fired into the courtyard of the apartment complex, showering at least sixty shots that injured four others and killed Makiyah. She died with the ice cream money still in her hand. Makiyah was the eighty-third homicide victim in D.C. in 2018 and the third child killed in July. Homicides were up 46 percent that year.[10]

A reporter for the *Post* described the tragic aftermath. "The shooting that killed Makiyah and wounded four others ended in hours of sirens and sobbing, and then came an eerie silence. By the time the sun began to set the next day, the crime-scene tape was gone. Police cruisers circled. But the playground remained empty."[11]

One more tragic note about what happens when the victim of a homicide is Black: in the past ten years, data from the country's fifty-two largest cities show that when a white person is killed, police arrest someone 63 percent of the time. When a Black person is killed, police arrest someone 47 percent of the time. That number is higher in the nation's capital—56 percent of homicides involving Black victims resulted in an arrest in Washington, D.C.—but is still far below the 69 percent for white homicide victims in the District.[12]

Just over a month after Makiyah was killed, another little girl in another underserved area of Washington, D.C., was shot in the ankle. Daziyah Ingraham is six years old and lives where gunshots are commonplace. Thankfully, she recovered from her wounds. Daziyah's mother doesn't believe her family was targeted. She has lived in the neighborhood all her life and says that gunshots "come with the territory." But other neighbors noted that the streetlights in the parking lot where Daziyah was shot hadn't worked all summer. At night, the neighborhood was pitch-black. Police had to use their flashlights to try to recover evidence. One resident said, "I just feel as though because we're east of the river, we get no type of help. We don't get the type of help you'd get if you lived up in Northwest."[13]

Children are alarmed not only about their personal safety; they also worry about their parents. One of my colleagues, Margery Rossi, tells how the idea of so many guns in her community has affected her two little boys. A few years ago

Margery's husband, Andy, was an elected member of a city council in a small city north of New York City. He attended weekly meetings that were televised and open to the public. Margery and her kids would occasionally watch the proceedings as they got ready for bed so the children could see their father on television.

One angry man in the community, who nursed long-standing grievances against the council, consistently showed up at meetings with new sets of circumstances and brought others to join the protests and to support him. The mayor and council agreed not to directly engage his vitriolic attacks, hoping that would soften his tone. Instead, he brought more people to the meetings, and became even louder and more confrontational.

After U.S. congresswoman Gabrielle Giffords and others were shot in Arizona in January 2011, Margery and Andy talked with their children, who were then seven and nine, about how incomprehensible it was for someone to do such a horrible thing. The next time the boys watched the city council meeting and listened to the angry attacks on the council, they grew fearful for their father's safety. Margery turned off the television and explained the difference between being boisterous and committing violent crimes. But the images of Gifford's shooting were seared into their minds, and they grew increasingly anxious whenever Andy went to council meetings. When Margery put them to bed on council meeting nights, they regularly prayed for their father's safety, hoping that "no one takes out a gun and shoots him."

Children in America should never have to worry about that; they should never have to pray such a prayer. Such a thing should not even cross their minds. In the industrialized world, only in America are children legitimately worried about gun violence. Their worries are collateral damage. What else would you call it? We are unique in the entire developed world with our laissez-faire approach to firearms. Otherwise intelligent leaders hardly give a passing thought to the fact that our country is swimming in unrestricted and unregulated guns. Our children are paying the price.

Fearful adults

It's not just children who carry this fear. All adults in the United States are "survivors" in some way. We see the constant stream of news reports about gun violence. We begin to fear for ourselves and our children. Whether we have lost someone close to us or have heard stories from those who did, we begin to feel vulnerable.

The reporting of the violence can even scare us into blaming "them"—whomever we consider to be the most dangerous. That fear prompts us to think no one is immune from the violence. We may begin to wonder whether we have a responsibility to buy a gun to keep our family safe. Maybe a gun would protect us? Maybe we'd be less anxious if we got a concealed carry permit? So we might buy a firearm, thinking it will help us protect those we love.

An individual's cycle of fear is not unlike what nations do. Individually and nationally, with domestic handguns and national weapons of war, we are doing what humankind has done for centuries. We are arming ourselves with more powerful weapons, both big and small, and teaching our men, women, and youth how to use firearms against "them." "Those people," whether real or perceived, individuals or nations, seem ubiquitous and menacing; we have to keep ourselves safe from "them." I have discovered that two of the most dangerous things in the world are a powerful, well-armed nation that is afraid and an individual who is afraid and is armed to the teeth.

That same kind of fear drives some adults straight to the gun store, where the vicious cycle of violence starts once more. But remember: the guns purchased for protection are twelve times more likely to be used against family members or other household members than to stop an intruder.[14] This statistic—which doesn't include suicides, other homicides, and crimes involving stolen guns—often gets buried underneath gundamentalist rhetoric.

Why does our fear of others provoke us to acquire such enormous levels of firepower? Why do law-abiding civilians need extended magazines for semiautomatic weapons filled with cop-killer bullets that can penetrate so-called bulletproof vests? Why do peaceable citizens need silencers for their guns, or grenades, or the latest assault weapon designed for use by the 101st Airborne or the Marine Corps? Is it not to assuage their fear? As words often attributed to the great soprano Marian Anderson go, "Fear is a disease that eats away at logic and makes human beings inhuman."

This permeating, dehumanizing fear is more collateral damage initiated by America's overwhelming number of guns, as well as the accompanying announcements of new gun attacks and assaults that pervade the news and drive the gullible to gun stores. This fear renders reason obsolete and sometimes prevents those of us who support common-sense gun legislation from speaking out because we fear for our own safety.

In 2018, the Virginia General Assembly authorized the issuance of a special interest license plate bearing the image of a broken heart and the words "Stop Gun Violence." By February 2019, hundreds of Virginians had submitted applications to receive the plates. Part of the revenue from these plates will go to support mental health services. I will not address the outrageous political roadblocks that gun zealots and their minions in the Virginia legislature erected to keep this bill from passing. But the First Amendment was a hurdle they could not overcome.

I was thrilled with the opportunity this legislation provided to get the word out. I encouraged many of my friends and contacts to purchase these plates. Thankfully, many of them did. But I was caught off guard when several of my good friends, who were strong advocates for reasonable gun laws and had written persuasive letters to the editor of the local paper and representatives in government, did not buy the license plates. One said, "We are in solid agreement with you and your cause. But we think displaying such a license plate could invite road rage and might put our families in danger."

Another remarked, "We have seen too many key scratches and acts of vandalism on cars whose bumper stickers or political signs suggested support for sensible gun control. We're sorry." So much for First Amendment rights to speak up and freely express one's ideas, one of the hallmarks of our democracy. These people are my good friends, and they are not timid Caspar Milquetoast kind of people. They are in the forefront of the struggle for justice and peace issues. But they were afraid to get license plates that included the words "Stop Gun Violence." It is apparent they were nervous because of the rhetoric and actions of a tiny segment of our population, and they are not alone.

I understand the reluctance of my good friends who do not want to take the risk of meeting some macho gun extremist on the highway or getting a nasty key scratch on their automobiles, but this fearful hesitancy to speak up and speak out is also part of America's collateral damage of living in the presence of 393 million guns: millions of Americans are afraid to speak their minds.

5

NOT JUST FOR SOLDIERS
PTSD, Suicide, and the Epidemic of Despair

ONE OF MY HEROES when I was a kid was my sister Harriet's boyfriend. Sandy Trout, a six-foot-four giant of a man, who fought in some of the heaviest fighting in World War II and was severely wounded in the Battle of the Bulge. When he returned home from the battlefield, he had a severe limp and had to use a cane. As a youngster, I dearly wanted to hear his war stories, but he refused to talk to me about them. The war movies I saw as a child made the war seem so exciting and even glamorous. But Sandy remained tight-lipped about all he had seen and done.

Today I understand Sandy's reluctance to speak. He had lived through the most brutal battle the United States fought in that war and the second deadliest battle in the country's history. Some 19,000 American soldiers lost their lives, 47,500 were wounded, and 23,000 were captured or missing in action. German casualties exceeded these numbers.

From what I know today about psychological trauma, it is clear that Sandy had post-traumatic stress disorder, or PTSD. The malady can be traced back to ancient civilization, with labels that demonstrate the way humans try to put a better spin on tragedy. During America's Civil War, it was called "soldier's heart." In the First World War it was termed "shell shock." In World War II it was called "battle fatigue." During the Korean War it was known as "operational exhaustion," and then PTSD after the Vietnam War, when the American Psychiatric Association added the term to its list of recognized mental disorders.[1] By whatever name, PTSD and its effects are the same.

Those who suffer from PTSD commonly experience nightmares or flashbacks of a particular event and experience it as if it's happening all over again. They feel alone and cut off from others and lose interest in things they used to care about. They are constantly on guard and are unable to concentrate. They may have fits of anger. Sleep is elusive, and they may have ongoing conflict with authority figures such as bosses, doctors, government officials, teachers, and ministers.

To deal with these predicaments, victims of PTSD often turn to alcohol or drugs, work obsessively to occupy their minds, or isolate themselves from loved ones. More than half of the 2.6 million Americans who fought in Iraq and Afghanistan experience physical or mental health problems arising from their time in combat. More than 40 percent of them experience ongoing mental and emotional problems. About 50 percent of soldiers know a service member who has attempted or committed suicide. Over one million "suffer from relationship problems and experience outbursts of anger, two key indicators of post-traumatic stress."[2]

For service members with PTSD, their bodies may be back home, but their minds and emotions are still in a war zone.

They cannot leave behind the trauma experienced half a world away, which makes it difficult to maintain relationships with spouses and children and move into new civilian neighborhoods. Fighting depression and suicide, those who were accustomed to living with guns at their sides in war zones feel they need them to protect themselves and their families. All too frequently, these guns are used to take not only their own lives but the lives of their spouses and children in murder-suicides.

PTSD

We usually associate PTSD with those in the military or veterans like Sandy. But in a nation swimming in guns, PTSD is now much more widespread. As stated earlier, more gun deaths have now occurred in our cities and towns than the number of military personnel lost on the battlefields of all U.S. wars since 1775. PTSD is not limited to soldiers or their families. It is collateral damage for thousands of citizens, especially those who live in urban America. Between 180,000 and 190,000 persons are directly injured by firearms every year. About 60,000 of those individuals suffer long-term depression or PTSD that lasts for years.[3]

Experiencing a mugging or robbery attempt, experiencing a home invasion, being near a shooting, being shot at whether you're hit or not, having family members and friends who are assaulted: these are likely to cause some level of PTSD. Children and youth are particularly vulnerable. School counselors in urban areas tell us that PTSD plagues children who hear gunshots at night.

The seventeen-year-old son of my friend Kenny Barnes was murdered by a young man who escaped from a halfway house. In the wake of his son's death, Kenny could have withdrawn from society, but he chose a different path. He chose to make his suffering redemptive by devoting himself to encouraging youth who live in violent neighborhoods. He is a frequent speaker at public schools in the nation's capital.

Kenny told me of one particular session in which he spoke to middle school kids in Washington, D.C. The entire student body met in the gymnasium; it was wall-to-wall kids, Kenny recalls. He told the young people about his son's murder. Then he asked them to stand if they knew someone who had been killed by a gun. The entire student body stood up.

It goes without saying that each of these kids is plagued by some level of post-traumatic stress. How can a youngster concentrate on math or social studies in the immediate aftermath of losing someone to gun violence? They are too busy trying to survive to be able to focus on schoolwork. PTSD is not just for soldiers. It affects kids and adults who are surrounded by guns, gunshots, and gun deaths.

Gun violence has a snowball effect that can be scientifically measured in education disparities, health outcomes, incarceration rates, and family instability. Researchers tell us that anxiety levels and cognitive functioning worsen among schoolchildren when a violent crime occurs within half a mile of their home.[4] As the number of firearms increases, the number of our citizens plagued by PTSD increases too.

Suicide

My dad broke his hip when he was in his eighties and had to use a walker. He could no longer drive and was dependent on neighbors for getting groceries and going to church or to the doctor. He was confined to his chair, and his only pleasure seemed to be listening to Lawrence Welk. My dad grew more depressed daily. Once he confided to me, "If I had a gun, I'd shoot myself." Thankfully, our family was spared that trauma.

One afternoon after lunch, Dad said, "I've never felt better in my life. I think I'll take a nap." He died in his sleep.

Dad was like so many older white men who are likely candidates for suicide. In the United States, older men of European descent have significantly higher suicide rates than any other demographic group.[5] Suicide is one of three types of death recently labeled by researchers as "diseases of despair": drug abuse, alcoholism, and suicide.[6] These diseases of despair affect young people as well. It is not unusual to hear of youngsters whose sweethearts informed them that their relationship was over, leading them to feel that life itself was over. "Why live?" they asked, and then took their own lives. And what of the star high school basketball player who missed two foul shots at the end of the game, costing his team the state championship? He was embarrassed, demoralized, and depressed. He let his friends down and could not stand the pain. His dad had a gun in his bedroom closet to protect the family. The young man got the gun and ended his agony.

Research tells us that if the guns had routinely been locked up, many suicide victims would be alive today. The easy availability of guns is an ever-present danger to those who are susceptible to impulsive acts, including suicide.

The American people are great believers in what makes the headlines. Many think it is a waste of time to read more than what appears below the large print. When it comes to gun deaths in most of our newspapers, the headlines seem reserved for mass shootings and terrorist attacks, the brutal slaying of schoolchildren, and the gunning down of worshipers while praying. More recently, shootings by or of police may make the top billing. But unless it is a famous person who takes his or her own life, suicides don't get much print. And without the headlines, there is little awareness of how common gun-related suicides really are. In fact, suicides make up two-thirds of all gun deaths.

Whenever we speak of guns in relation to suicide, we are in the company of myths that need to be dispelled. One of the most erroneous beliefs is that suicides are planned over many days, weeks, or even years. While that may be true in some instances, empirical evidence suggests that the suicidal act often takes place in a moment of brief but intense vulnerability. When a gun is used, unlike other methods, it requires less preparation and planning. Nearly half (48 percent) of suicide-attempt patients reported that fewer than twenty minutes elapsed between their first thought of suicide and their actual attempt.[7]

The American Association for Suicidology reports that 31,000 suicides occur annually in the United States. For every one of these deaths, they estimate six more people try to kill themselves but do not succeed. According to this estimate, there are now 4.47 million American survivors of suicide, and each year produces 186,000 more.[8] Add to this huge number those who suffer PTSD from gun violence, and you see that we are a nation of wounded citizens who are hurting and grieving. We are beginning to take this collateral damage for granted. We have chosen to inflict this despair on our citizens because we are trying so hard to live with 393 million guns.

Those who attempt suicide in ways other than with a gun often have some time to reconsider mid-attempt, and may stop or summon help to be rescued. Many methods themselves often fail, even in the absence of a rescue.[9] But suicide by gun is different. Bullets usually don't provide second chances. Sit with this statistic for a moment: Fifty-eight people will kill themselves today. More than half will use a gun.

Just as handguns are the most widely used instruments of murder, so they are also the most common and effective instrument for suicide. Rifles and shotguns are also lethal, but handguns are much easier to use and therefore more effective.

Lifesavers

So what can we do? First, we can take away from a depressed person the means of killing oneself. That act is a lifesaver. As one psychiatrist observed, "suicidal urges typically wax and wane, so it follows that difficult access to a lethal means of self-destruction may favor survival."[10] Several colleagues, in support of his thesis, cited England and Wales' success in curbing suicide by reducing the lethality of the most common means at that time—domestic coal gas.

For a time, coal gas, regularly used in cooking stoves, was the most common means of suicide. To reduce suicides by coal gas, this toxic gas was replaced by nontoxic natural gas. Studies conducted after the switch found that "British [suicide] rates have remained reduced for the past fifteen years, and . . . there has been an almost one-to-one correspondence between the reduction of suicides and the number of people who had used coal gas in prior years."[11]

Today, California, Washington, Oregon, Indiana, and Connecticut have statutes that allow for the removal of America's most effective means of suicide—a firearm—and thus save countless lives. The gun violence restraining order can be used to temporarily take guns away from someone a judge deems a threat to themselves or others. Lawmakers in fourteen other states and the District of Columbia have proposed similar measures.[12] Such good laws came into being because people like you cared about their brothers and sisters and asked, "What can we do to stop the madness?" Their love and imagination have saved many lives.

More conversations, more information

As we saw in chapter 2, facts matter. To get to the facts, we need research. And suicide is one area that calls for significant research, as well as significant conversation. We'll look more at the question of research in chapter 9. Today, the Centers for Disease Control collect data from police and coroner reports and death certificates on every gun death, but this data covers only eighteen states. Compare that with the National Highway Traffic Safety Administration's Fatality Analysis Reporting System, which receives extensive details within thirty days of every fatal crash on public roads: everything from the time and location of the accident to weather conditions to the role, if any, of alcohol and drugs. Partly because of this diligent tracking system and resulting educational and public safety initiatives, the fatality rate from car crashes has dropped by about a third over the last twenty years.[13] Could the same diligence bring down the number of suicides? Public health officials answer, "Yes, without a doubt."

Unfortunately, Congress has mandated ignorance on research about guns and gun deaths, making it easy for gun rights groups to manipulate conversations. Gundamentalists assert that having a gun near a depressed person is no cause for alarm, and they advocate legal action against psychiatrists who ask despondent patients if there is a gun in the home. They contend that such an inquiry is a political question, not a medical one.

Consider the questions physicians ask their patients about the use of tobacco and alcohol and opioids, or about seat belt use. I believe it is a doctor's responsibility to advise patients about *any* risk to health. Suggesting that doctors have conversations with children and youth about wearing bike helmets or clicking a seat belt but *not* about the safe storage of firearms should be seen as malpractice.

Better data is a good place to start. According to *Harvard Public Health* magazine, "Ultimately, the goal is to transcend politics—which is why those who have lost loved ones to gun suicide should have the last word." In their illuminating report, they give that word to Wendy Tapp, the mother of nineteen-year-old Ryan Tapp, who killed himself with a handgun in 2011. "Ryan is my baby," she said. "I remember once telling him, 'If anything happens to you, I would cease to exist.' And that's what it feels like. It's a pain like no other. I would encourage open conversation—actually talking about it. Preventing just one person from going through what I went through and will go through for the rest of my life—that would be enough for me."[14]

I served as the interfaith chair of the Million Mom March in 2000. One million concerned Americans met on the Washington Mall to protest gun violence, and hundreds of thousands participated in satellite marches throughout the country. There were speeches, prayers, and songs led by amateur musicians and rock stars. One of the best speeches I heard was by a young widow named Courtney Love.

> Six years ago on April 7, my husband, Kurt Cobain, shot himself to death. Suicide is a permanent solution to a temporary emotion. If you've ever lived with somebody with depression, you know how they suffer. But you should also know that there is help. Depression is treatable. So it is one of the greatest tragedies on earth that of the 32,000 gun deaths every year in America, 17,000 are those who killed themselves. [These are 2000 figures. As noted, in 2017, gun deaths approached 40,000. Over 23,000 of these were suicides.] . . . In a moment of desperation and chaos, life is ended because a gun was handy, and near, and probably unregistered.

There are those who say, "Oh, please have a gun for protection," but I know better. Suicide is five times more likely in a house with a gun than in a house without one. . . . Ask a child like my little girl, Frances, who will never have her father hold her hand as she walks to school, or teach her to play guitar. Ask her if it is good protection.

And that's why I'm here. If we register guns, if we license gun owners, if we check for criminal records and for mental illness, then we will make it harder for people to buy guns, and then we will save countless lives.[15]

The NRA not only disputes but disparages remarks like Love's. They deny that gun availability increases the chance of suicide, stating, "If a person is determined to kill himself, he will find a way." In reality, the NRA casts the link between suicide and guns as something of a virtue. An NRA fact sheet about suicide and firearms says, "Gun owners are notably self-reliant and exhibit a willingness to take definitive action when they believe it to be in their own self-interest. Such action may include ending their own life when the time is deemed appropriate."[16]

This claim makes it crystal clear that the NRA's interest is not in preventing suicide but in maintaining their power and selling guns.

Race, suicide, and homicides

Gun deaths among whites are far more likely to be suicides, while among African Americans gun deaths are far more likely to be homicides. In rural America especially, many white people see guns as part of their way of life and not a great threat to social stability. Many African Americans, however, fear gun crime and tend to be strong advocates for gun control measures. We will look at racism and gun violence in later chapters. For now, let's look specifically at suicide as it relates to race.

Janet Massolo, who is white, lost her fifteen-year-old daughter, Shannon, to suicide. After one of Shannon's friends shot herself to death, Massolo recalls Shannon asking her, "How could anything get that bad?" But six months later, Shannon shot herself with her father's handgun.

Shannon had grown up learning how to handle guns. Her parents had taken her to shooting ranges, where she learned how to shoot. In an interview with the *Washington Post*, Massolo said, "The mind-set out here is that we use guns for hunting, for target shooting, to keep the family safe. If you want to keep the family safe, and you have a mental illness in the family, then lock your guns up for a while, or give them away for a while. We're not saying give them away forever. We don't want to take the gun away."[17]

The gun was a gift to Shannon's father from his father-in-law, a former police officer, and had sentimental value. Massolo said, "That's something we have dealt with. We taught Shannon how to kill herself, but we were trying to teach her how to be safe." After the suicide inquiry, Massolo's husband retrieved the gun from the police. She won't look at it, the *Post* reported, "but her husband won't part with it."[18] Massolo now works at a suicide prevention center.

Consider as well the response of Shanda Smith, who is Black, and who sees guns very differently. Twenty years ago her two children were shot to death while driving to a Christmas party at their church. Her nineteen-year-old son Rodney was home from college for the holidays. He had borrowed a relative's car to drive to the party. His sister, Volante, and two friends were also in the car. As they neared the church, someone ran up to the car and shot Rodney and Volante. The killings were determined to be cases of mistaken identity. "[My kids] were right where they needed to be," Smith said, "but somebody had access to a gun."

Although Smith knows many people who have suffered from gun-related homicides, she observed that victims' families don't buy guns as a solution. "That's a difference in the African American community," she told the *Washington Post*. "We don't teach our kids to go hunting and shoot. We don't have guns in our homes." As Sean Joe, an expert on suicide at the University of Michigan, says succinctly: "Increased access to firearms increases both suicides and murders."[19]

The questions that never end

The media generally do not cover suicides. Perhaps they regard a news article on a suicide as an invasion of privacy. Or perhaps we can say the media have bought into the NRA line quoted above that describes suicide as a "self-reliant" act of "appropriate self-interest."

It is past time for us to come to grips with the fact that, regardless of whether deaths are by suicide or by murder, keeping a handgun in our home places everyone in the house at a far greater risk. I have had family members and two close friends succeed in taking their own lives. I can testify that the pain of asking unanswerable questions is never over. The whys never cease, nor do the countless wonderings come to an end. The what ifs and if onlys continue to haunt those closest to the victim. Surviving family members not only suffer the trauma of losing a loved one but are at higher risk themselves for emotional problems and the temptation to take their own lives.

As noted earlier, so many people choose to buy a gun for protection: to protect themselves and their families from people who might want to harm them. But when a problem arises—the loss of a job, an illness, depression, trauma, an accident, an argument with a family member—and a gun is nearby, people think about using it. When guns are in the vicinity, they become a possibility.

6

OUR TEACHERS' ARMS
Guns in Public Spaces

CONCEALED **CARRY LEGISLATION** permits individuals to carry concealed weapons. All fifty U.S. states allow some form of concealed carry. Some states only issue permits to residents of their state, while others issue permits to nonresidents as well. Still others have reciprocal agreements by which they honor each other's permit.

In the wake of the concealed carry movement, a thriving business for paraphernalia has developed. Websites sell special vests, jackets, T-shirts, and even underwear for holding weapons. One company makes boxer briefs with a holster in the back, which they call "compression concealment shorts." (Writer David Sedaris suggests calling them "gunderpants."[1] Actually, hiding a lethal weapon in one's underpants could be dangerous. I read of a man who died after sitting on a gun he had hidden under his seat cushion. The bullet severed his femoral artery.)

All this paraphernalia—which increases one's readiness to pull out a gun at a moment's notice—does not lend itself to building an open, caring community. Moreover, everyone's First Amendment right to free speech without fear of coercion is threatened when guns are present. Even when guns are concealed, the possibility exists that a volatile person with a history of violent acts might be carrying a pistol, only God knows where.

When guns proliferate in public spaces, the quality of our social interactions changes, or even disintegrates. We won't know the extent of the collateral damage done by the expanding presence of guns for some time, but let's look at some of the issues that emerge when guns are taken or smuggled into schools, businesses, and churches. We'll also look at some of the tragically bizarre stories resulting from the abundance of guns in public and private spaces.

Guns in schools and universities

After the catastrophic murders of seventeen high school students and teachers at Marjory Stoneman Douglas High School in Florida, the *Washington Post* undertook a yearlong analysis of school shootings. The study revealed that beginning with Columbine High School in 1999, more than 187,000 students in at least 193 primary or secondary schools have experienced a shooting on campus during school hours. Campus shootings happened in thirty-six states, in both big cities and small towns. Sixty-eight of these schools employed a police officer or security guard, but only once did a resource officer stop an active shooter.[2]

At the time of this writing, the U.S. secretary of education, Betsy DeVos, appointed by President Trump as chair of a panel on school safety, was planning to lead a national study on gun violence in schools. The panel was established in the wake of the high school massacre in Parkland, Florida. However, guns themselves are not going to be part of the conversation. In case you missed that, let me say it again: a panel was going to study school and gun violence, but the effects of guns were not going to be considered by the participants.[3]

How can this be? As I argued earlier, this is like conducting research on communicable diseases but refusing to discuss the flu. DeVos is firmly in the gundamentalist camp and its core belief that "guns don't kill people; people kill people." Our nation's secretary of education, in lockstep with the corporate gun lobby, thinks more guns in more teachers' hands will solve the problem of gun violence in schools.[4] Her ideology is but one more demonstration of how the uncritical, unthinking acceptance of 393 million unregulated guns in the country spawns an extremist devotion to weapons.

Data on school shootings should be thoroughly examined by federal and state governments and school boards before they make knee-jerk decisions to arm our educators. The numbers suggest that if teachers are armed, there is a good chance they would end up shooting their own students—those who just happen to bring a gun to school for their own "show and tell" or to keep a bully at bay. Far more effective measures for school safety would be for gun-owning parents to lock up their guns and keep them away from their children. The *Washington Post* reports that since 1999, the shooters in at least 145 acts of gun violence at primary and secondary schools have been under the age of eighteen. For the 105 cases that identified the weapon's source, 80 percent involved guns taken from the child's home or the home of relatives or friends. Yet just four adults have been convicted for failing to lock up the guns used.[5]

The *Post* writes, "Discussions about how to curb shootings at American schools have centered on arming teachers or improving mental health treatment, banning military-style rifles or strengthening background checks. But if children as young as 6 did not have access to guns in the first place, . . . two-thirds of all the school shootings over the past two decades could not have happened."[6] Children are bringing guns to school at alarming rates because adults are not acting like adults and locking up their guns. Denying access to guns is one of the simplest yet most critical factors for safe schools.

Like lemmings over a cliff, Secretary DeVos and her ilk are ready to give a sympathetic ear to anyone who will propose any cockamamie scheme to put more guns into people's hands, even into the hands of three-year-old children. Here's that story: Two of the most powerful gun rights advocates in Virginia—Philip Van Cleave, president of the Virginia Citizens Defense League, and Larry Pratt, executive director emeritus of Gun Owners of America—expressed their support for arming toddlers, which the proposal (a fictitious one suggested by comedian Sacha Baron Cohen) referred to as "kinderguardians," and for making available "gunny rabbits" and "uzicorns" that hide concealed pistols.[7] These are not ordinary gun lovers. These are dedicated gun zealots. In January 2018, Van Cleave led the fight in the Virginia legislature to defeat a bill that would make it illegal to give a loaded gun to a five-year-old child. During the legislative debates, the sentiment was often raised that the Second Amendment does not include an age restriction.

In 2015, the Texas legislature passed a law that allows students to bring concealed handguns on campus. That decision caused Daniel Hamermesh, a popular economics professor emeritus who had taught at the University of Texas for over twenty years, to resign his position. In a letter to the president of the university, he said, "The risk that a disgruntled student might bring a gun into the classroom and start shooting at me has been substantially enhanced by this concealed-carry law."

Out of a concern for self-protection, Hamermesh planned to spend part of next year at a university in Australia, "where, among other things, this risk seems lower." Ironically, the law took effect on August 1, 2016, the fiftieth anniversary of the first U.S. mass shooting on a college campus, which took place at the University of Texas.[8]

With some students carrying concealed weapons, Hamermesh reasoned that the free and open atmosphere where students and faculty could speak with passion on any subject without fearing retaliation was now poisoned. From sad experience, we know impassioned arguments can turn deadly when a gun is nearby. As noted earlier, the latest data show that people only rarely use guns for self-defense.

Guns in businesses

Before Starbucks displayed signs at the entrances to their coffee shops that guns were not welcome, I learned of a woman who, as she walked into a Starbucks, spotted a guy with a gun at his side. She never broke stride, just made an abrupt U-turn and walked right out. Perhaps incidents like that prompted Starbucks to prohibit guns in their establishments, or maybe the CEO or someone in management had a friend or family member who was shot. Whatever the reason, Starbucks did not consider guns to be inanimate or friendly instruments to have around while customers sipped their lattes. Additional businesses, including Chipotle, Panera, Sonic, Chili's, and Target, followed suit, putting up a simple sign on their front doors stating that guns were not welcome in their establishments. I'm glad they did, because the presence of a gun does not make everybody feel safe; it terrifies many.

The United States Supreme Court has declared that individuals have a right to buy guns and use them, even to carry them around concealed or in the open. But those of us who don't want them around also have a right to limit their presence. The Second Amendment itself carries with it the idea that gun ownership is to be "well regulated"—that is, there are reasonable limits to one's right to keep and bear arms. Remember: it is the only amendment that has a built-in regulation.

It takes a long time and endless repetition of the truth for powerful myths to die. Ergo, it takes courage to put a bumper sticker or license plate on one's car or a sign on one's church or place of business. In the meantime, I say hooray for those businesses that have shown a measure of bravery in making a much-needed social statement. If America's silent majority raised their voices and joined these courageous leaders, we would see change in America's gun laws. I'm certain that management in those companies had their doubts and fears as well before they made a decision to act, but despite their doubts and fears, they took a risk and raised their voices for the public good.

And how about churches? Unfortunately, we find that the secular business community often has more courage than faith communities who claim to be guided by the Holy Scriptures.

Guns in churches

The Lord Jesus does not call us to be a mirror reflecting the norms of our society; rather, he calls us to be a light from God to show the world what love, justice, and a good caring community looks like.

For years, the consensus among Christians has been that guns, except those carried by law enforcement, do not belong in houses of worship. In 2016, the General Assembly of the Presbyterian Church (USA), asked its member churches and agencies to consider placing signs at their doors that state "Guns do not belong in God's house." Dozens of churches took the risk and placed such signs at their entrances. It is a compelling congregational witness that members will not allow their sanctuary or environs to become an armed camp. Yet it still is a risk.

I worship at a Presbyterian church in Harrisonburg, Virginia, a progressive town surrounded by gun country. There was a palpable fear in my own church when our session (the elders and pastor who make up the governing body) debated whether to place signs on our doors indicating to all that firearms were not welcome in our house of worship. Despite the expressed fear that this was too big a risk to take, the session voted to post the following at each of our doors: "In respect for the safety of all, this is a gun-free building."

Those who were opposed to the placement of any sign argued that placing such notices on our doors might be seen as an invitation to mentally unstable persons to come in and start shooting. They maintained that angry people or those with mental illnesses might see such a sign as an indication that our church was a "soft target." This very same argument was voiced hundreds of times in congregations across the country by those whose ultimate motivation was fear over *what could possibly happen* instead of faith that expressed *what should be happening* in God's house.

God's children should never be afraid to take a few risks and stand up and be counted for what is right and what ought to be. In God's long run, the truth will prevail. We can count on that. It is a promise from God, and it is a joy to participate even in a small way in God's victory. But faithfulness requires some risks, at least every now and then. After all, we follow Jesus, the crucified but risen Lord.

Gun-free spaces

I'd wager that many congregations afraid to place such signs on their property would be shocked to learn that their fearful reluctance puts them in lockstep with proposals from the NRA, gun manufacturers, the extremist far right, and President Trump, all of whom insist on the need to place armed guards in our classrooms and places of worship. (Remember: in sixty-eight of the schools in which mass shootings took place, a police officer or security guard had been hired for protection; only once did a resource officer stop an active shooter.)

For decades, gundamentalists have shouted from the housetops the very same message about gun-free zones, saying that they make these places "soft targets." They contend that the only way a place of worship, coffee shop, other business, or school can be safe is to have people armed with powerful guns to protect themselves and others. It is a myth but a powerful one, and it sells many more guns and comforts the fearful with false hope.

Why, then, haven't more businesses, stores, schools, eating establishments, and houses of worship put up signs prohibiting guns on their premises? The short answer is they are afraid to do so. Who are they afraid of? It is not the silent majority of gun owners in America who support background checks on all guns sold and other sensible gun laws. They are not the problem. The nation is afraid of the tiny segment of gundamentalists whose extremism about taking guns everywhere places them only one synapse away from shooting someone who might suggest their firearm should have a regulation or two placed on it. They are the ones with the angriest speech; they are the ones most likely to pull the trigger on another person without good cause; they are the ones most likely to issue a death threat to the owners of stores, principals of schools, or religious leaders for displaying a sign stating that guns are not welcome on their premises. This tiny group of extremists perpetuates fear and holds the entire nation hostage to the mistaken idea that those with the guns are the ones who make the rules.

So let's say for the moment that none of the rationale in this chapter has convinced you to be concerned about carrying weapons in public spaces. Let's say you think we need to be realistic about the dangerous times in which we're living—that we should admit that arming teachers, while not ideal, might be our best option. We must protect our children at all costs, you might say. We need to be realistic. The fundamental question is . . .

Would it work?

Just how safe would schools and businesses and houses of worship be if we figured out how to arm adults to protect these spaces? Two New York City police officers shot at a gun-wielding assailant near the Empire State Building in 2012. They killed him, and in the process wounded nine innocent bystanders.[9] This prompted the police commissioner to request an analysis of officers' "hit ratios." The study revealed for the years 1998–2006, "the average hit ratio for officers involved in a shooting where the subject does not fire back was 30 percent." And when a subject fires at officers, the hit ratio falls to 18 percent.[10]

These findings spark several questions for those willing to pay attention. NYPD officers are some of the best-trained police in the world. They are required to spend hours on firing ranges to maintain their shooting proficiency. Every firearms instructor I know repeats an old adage ad infinitum: "The ability to hit one's target with a firearm depends on one's training and continuing practice." In other words, *you use it or you lose it*. The training the NYPD police receive is far more extensive than anything that could ever be provided for teachers, baristas, bartenders, parishioners, or volunteers. If we are going to arm any of our teachers or church ushers, we must insist they make regular trips to firing ranges. Think about that for a moment.

Also reflect on the fact that 21 percent of law enforcement officers killed with a handgun were shot with their own weapon.[11]

And now consider this: Even with training, is it realistic to expect your average second-grade teacher or one of the people who take the offering on Sunday to have a better hit ratio than members of the NYPD? The hit ratios of professional law enforcement mentioned above do not convince me that we should arm teachers in the classroom or greeters in the church lobby.

After the shooting at Marjory Stoneman Douglas in Florida, the *Washington Post* reported that President Trump "reiterated his belief that arming teachers would prevent school shootings" like that one. He lauded a Texas program that puts armed marshals in schools. Mass shooters are cowards, he said; "they're not going [to attack] a school when they know they're going to come out dead."[12]

Criminologist Adam Lankford, who studies mass shootings at the University of Alabama, has a different take. He says, "A significant subset of these offenders have specifically targeted government buildings and military facilities"—that is, places where armed opposition is essentially expected. As the *Post* notes, "Shooters intending to go out in a 'blaze of glory,' either by their own hand or via a shootout with police, are unlikely to be deterred by the presence of more 'good guys' with guns. The data on mass shootings would appear to bear this out."[13]

Researchers agree that "other policies are much better suited to reducing the toll of mass shooting deaths" than arming people in public places. Universal background checks and bans on high-capacity magazines and assault weapons are among their recommendations, which we'll look at in more detail in chapter 10.[14] It's safe to say that arming teachers and cashiers and greeters at houses of worship opens up Pandora's box. Too many things can go wrong.

Related to the question of guns in public spaces is the reality of irresponsible behavior by far too many gun owners. Stories of recklessness with weapons abound, creating a bizarre collage of facts about guns that should give anyone pause.

Files of the absurd

I was in my twenties before I ever heard of Uncle Charlie. One summer day, exploring the second floor of the big barn behind my aunt's house in Rockford, Illinois, I discovered a portrait of a good-looking, red-haired young man. Curiously, it was positioned faceup, directly underneath a roost for pigeons. My curiosity was piqued. I knew there must be a story that accompanied this portrait. Did anyone really deserve such indignity?

I learned that Uncle Charlie had a great fondness for alcohol and an equal love for poker and "playing the ponies," as my aunt put it. I'm speaking not of a drink or two or a bet or two but of addiction and irresponsible behavior. He essentially gambled away two large family farms. The locale of his portrait began to make some sense.

Irresponsible behavior takes many forms. One sees it every day as reckless drivers of cars and motorcycles weave in and out of traffic at great speed on crowded highways. Every school principal works with children and youth who engage in irrational behavior. Every police department and courthouse stands ready to confront irresponsible behavior.

Most hunters, including the people I hunted with for more than fifty years, are very careful with their guns and ammunition. Still, in the past few years, at least six gun owners have been shot by their dogs: the animals walked on the gun when it was on the ground or rested on the back seat of their cars or boats.[15]

It is no secret that guns are frequently misused or handled recklessly. We should be able to agree it is careless and irresponsible behavior to leave a gun loaded, unlocked, and unattended anywhere, but especially in places that children frequent. Shamefully, we have a long way to go before locking up loaded guns becomes a norm in America. We are living with innumerable instances of irresponsible behavior with guns. When we talk about guns and their use and misuse, there are never-ending records of absurd thinking and careless behavior that have led to unspeakable tragedies. What follows is a brief peek at stories of bizarre shootings. I collect these in what I call my "absurdity file," which is two inches thick.

A frightened woman from Oregon wrote Anne Landers in 2001:

> Dear Ann:
> My husband and I recently took our 4-year-old daughter with us on a short vacation. We rented a room at a lovely resort. We were shocked when the manager phoned to say he needed to come to our room to retrieve a loaded handgun in the unlocked nightstand drawer in the bedroom where our daughter was sleeping.
>
> We had been using the room for half a day before the manager called. The gun was left behind by the previous guest, who was an off-duty corrections officer. How could any professional be so careless?
>
> Please caution your readers to inspect all drawers, closets, and cupboards when they enter their hotel room or rented condo. You never know who used the place before you and what they might have left behind. —*Frightened in Oregon*

Ann replied: "Bless you for a letter that could save lives. I never would have thought to do this. Take note, readers. This could be a life-saving wake up call."[16]

"How could any professional be so careless?" asked the woman. But literally thousands of times every year in the United

States, gun owners misplace or forget their guns. Owning a fire-arm of any sort calls for extraordinary responsibility, and one cannot be cavalier about an instrument whose purpose is to kill. Far too often, even high-ranking law enforcement officers and legislators who should know better handle their guns in a casual manner. A casual attitude about one's firearm makes it all the more dangerous for gun owners, their families, their col-leagues at work, and for the general public.

Missouri lawmakers have long supported concealed carry almost anywhere and anytime. An editorial in the *Kansas City Star* asked if the right extends to the men's room in the Missouri Capitol basement. That is where a staffer for former House Speaker Tim Jones left a loaded handgun on top of a toilet pa-per dispenser.[17] Is it unreasonable to insist that all gun owners know where their weapons are *at all times*? I can understand misplacing one's glasses or car keys. I do it all the time. But for the life of me I cannot understand how one can misplace a 9mm handgun. How is that possible?

In 2015, Alvin Krongard, former executive director of the CIA under George W. Bush, did just that. He was arrested try-ing to bring a 9mm handgun with five rounds of ammunition past security at Baltimore/Washington International Airport. He said he must have just grabbed the wrong bag at home. "I didn't even know I was carrying a gun," he said.[18]

A replica of a suicide vest was found in a checked bag at a Texas airport; a block of inert explosives was discovered in a carry-on bag at a Florida airport; hand grenades were found in luggage at airports across the country. And 3,957 firearms were discovered by Transportation Security Administration agents at airport checkpoints in 2017. Some 35 percent of them were loaded. The *Washington Post* reported, "That's up roughly 17 percent from 2016, when 3,391 firearms were found at checkpoints, TSA said. And the number of firearms found has risen steadily since TSA began tracking it in 2005, when 660 firearms were found."[19]

TSA officers are skilled at confiscating shampoo from carry-on luggage at airports to keep the public safe, but other government officials regulate what few good gun laws we do have in reckless ways. From February 2016 to March 2017, the state of Florida failed to conduct a background check for hundreds of thousands of concealed carry permits because the employee responsible for the job could not log into the system. Not one application was denied. Not one. Who knows how many people today are walking around with concealed carry permits that should have been denied?[20] Just to jog your memory, Stephen Paddock had a concealed carry permit. Remember him? He was the man who killed fifty-eight people and wounded more than eight hundred in the Las Vegas massacre in 2017.

There is a price to pay when gunowners forget where their guns are. Twelve-year-old Jacob Larson of Palm Harbor, Florida, came across a gun in his family's home and shot himself in the head. His parents told the police that they had forgotten they even had the gun.[21]

In Portland, Oregon, a McDonald's restaurant botched an order. Lofton Lane was so angry about this that he fired nineteen rounds into the establishment.[22]

In Michigan, "a six-year feud came to a deadly end during a church service . . . just as the priest was preparing to distribute communion. . . . The gunman stood up and yelled 'Yes, I am here,' then shot Gjek Isufaj, 38, in the back of the head. He shot Isufaj several more times, then fired into the air and yelled 'I done what I was supposed to do.'"[23]

In Georgia, "an antique .38-caliber pistol accidently discharged as it was being handled by Rep. Bob Barr during a reception. . . . Georgia gun lobbyist Bruce Widener said . . . he had removed the magazine from the 1908 Colt but did not clear the chamber before handing the weapon to Barr, a board member of the National Rifle Association."[24]

In Pennsylvania, twenty-year-old Randy Johnson was spinning a loaded gun on his finger just before it accidentally went off. The bullet hit his girlfriend in the abdomen. While police were treating the woman, he panicked and shot the gun a second time.[25]

Also in Pennsylvania, an eight-year-old girl died after her six-year-old brother accidentally shot her in the eye with a BB gun.[26]

In New York City, nine-year-old Taniqua Hall clambered onto a kitchen counter looking for some peanut butter to fix a midnight snack. Instead she found a loaded .22-caliber revolver, which she accidentally fired at her own chest. She died as her twelve-year-old cousin looked on helplessly.[27]

In Washington, D.C., a three-year-old boy was "in critical condition . . . after he was shot with a . . . semiautomatic handgun that belongs to his father, a U.S. Secret Service officer [who] . . . works the nights shift guarding the White House. . . . [A] spokesman for the Secret Service said that all officers are issued a lock for their guns. 'When you are off duty, it's supposed to be locked,' he said."[28]

In Indiana, a man fatally shot his nine-year-old daughter in the head while teaching his two sons about gun safety. He was telling his sons about the dangers of playing with guns when his daughter walked into the room and was killed.[29]

In 1996, a man who lost a Bible quoting contest killed the man who had bested him in their competition. Gabriel Taylor and the suspected shooter were comparing their Bible knowledge outside an apartment complex, each quoting different versions of the same passage. The suspect retrieved his Bible and realized he was wrong. He said that Taylor knew more than he did, and that made him mad. He threatened to kill Taylor before the night was out. He left with two other people who witnessed the exchange.[30]

Bullets fired into the air in celebration, usually on New Year's Eve and the Fourth of July, have killed at least forty people since 1985 in Los Angeles County, California, alone.[31] My friend Joe Jaskolka of Philadelphia, who fortunately recovered, spent weeks in a hospital on life support after being hit in the head by a bullet that was fired up into the air and, unsurprisingly, came back down.

A television station in Detroit reported that a fifty-year-old man was in his home when he saw a cockroach. The man, who uses a wheelchair, threw his shoe at the insect. However, the shoe had a revolver inside. When it fell out, it discharged and shot him in his foot.[32]

Some of the most heart-wrenching stories of gun deaths occur when curious children discover a firearm that is loaded and unlocked in their home or in a neighbor's home and accidentally kill themselves or their playmates. A survey of parents who own guns found that they were far more likely to place caps over electrical outlets than to lock up their firearms. A researcher at the University of North Carolina School of Medicine collected data on safety practices from nearly three hundred parents who turned up in emergency departments and had children under seven. As she described, "When I designed the study, I hypothesized that people who exercised good general safety habits would also have good firearm safety habits as well." Overall, the parents had good safety habits—"99 percent had a smoke alarm, 72 percent put caps on outlets and 72 percent put poisonous substances out of their children's reach. But when it came to guns, the picture was not so positive: 57 percent said they did not store their guns in locked compartments and 36 percent said they kept their guns loaded." The researcher noted that the potential for accidents is not the only reason guns should be locked away. Suicide rates are high among teens.[33]

Even reading these bizarre events will not convince some gundamentalists to lock up their firearms. One told me, "A gun that is not loaded and unlocked is like a car in the garage without gas."

We need to consider the presence of guns and examine the unexpected worst-case scenarios for every single gun's use. According to an analysis of figures from the National Crime Victimization Survey, people "successfully" defended themselves with a gun in only 0.9 percent of crimes from 2007 to 2011. David Hemenway, who led the analysis, asserted that "the risks of owning a gun outweigh the benefits of having one in the rare case where you might need to defend yourself." As he told *Here and Now*'s Robin Young, "The average person . . . has basically no chance in their lifetime ever to use a gun in self-defense. . . . But . . . every day, they have a chance to use the gun inappropriately. They have a chance, they get angry. They get scared."[34]

COUNT THE COST
The Economic Toll of Gun Violence

AS THE VICTIMS of gun violence are taken either to the morgue or to a hospital, collateral damage continues its toll. One of the ways it exacts a cost—literally—is on the American economy.

Even if there were no economic cost to gun violence, the sheer fact of the human lives lost should be enough to make us change our laws and our conversations about guns. Once, when I spoke at a luncheon in Arlington, Virginia, I was intrigued that several in attendance were demonstrably more concerned about the yearly economic cost of gun violence to Virginia than they were about the actual number of Virginians who lost their lives by firearms. I wish that weren't the case. I wish people would be more concerned about the human costs than about the economic ones. Yet if the loss of life and the awful pain incurred by family and friends does not move someone, perhaps the staggering amount of money that gun violence costs taxpayers will.

For every person killed, injured, or simply threatened by a gun, there are enormous economic costs to individuals, families, schools, religious institutions, hospitals, government agencies, workplaces, stores, and businesses. In 2007, Seung Hui Cho, a college senior, brutally gunned down thirty-two precious lives at Virginia Tech. As columnist Petula Dvorak asked, "What does allowing a mentally ill young man to legally buy two guns and an arsenal of magazines cost the rest of us in dollar terms? About $48.2 million." Dvorak cites research by the Center for American Progress, which dug into the costs of the attack by "sifting through the legal bills, university staffing costs, police costs, hospital bills and autopsy receipts that kept piling up long after the candlelight vigils ended."[1]

Dvorak writes, "The $48.2 million tab for the two-hour shooting rampage was picked up by local, state and federal taxpayers, the public university system, parents and students. That's a huge chunk of a state budget, and any other event that cost this much would get unblinking scrutiny."[2]

After an entire first-grade class in Newtown, Connecticut, was mowed down by an assault rifle in the hands of a mentally unstable young man, the economic costs to Newtown included tearing down the old school and building a new one for $50 million. There were too many raw memories to leave that structure standing to torture its citizens for years to come.[3]

As I noted earlier, the number of suicides involving firearms has helped to push U.S. gun deaths to their highest rate in more than twenty years. Nearly forty thousand people were killed in shootings in 2017. In addition, each year at least eighty thousand people survive gunshot wounds. They experience a range of injuries, including life-altering paralysis. In all, this means that well over one hundred thousand times every year, bullets pierce the soft tissue of human bodies—in one country alone.[4]

And what is the financial cost to society of all that carnage? *Mother Jones* magazine, working with researcher Ted Miller, has estimated it to be $229 billion per year. The price tag includes medical treatment, court costs, prison for perpetrators, lost wages for victims, crime victim compensation, funeral and burial expenses, and other economic impacts. According to *Mother Jones*, that amounts to $700 for every person in the country: "Direct costs account for $8.6 billion—including long-term prison costs for people who commit assault and homicide using guns, which at $5.2 billion a year is the largest direct expense. Even before accounting for the more intangible costs of the violence, in other words, the average cost to taxpayers for a single gun homicide in America is nearly $400,000."[5]

About 87 percent of the direct costs fall to government budgets—as in, taxpayers. The indirect costs—to victims and their families and communities, and to taxpayers—are difficult to measure. Either way, gun violence is an expensive burden on society.

Medical expenses

Back in 1975, when I started asking participants in seminars how many knew someone who had been shot or killed by a gun, only a few raised their hands. When I ask the same question today, as I lead seminars across the country, many more hands are raised. In fact, according to some reports, nearly 45 percent of Americans know someone who has been shot.[6] I also often ask seminar participants, "What is the major contributor to this enormous economic price tag?" A frequent answer is "medical expenses." That is a good guess. As we will see in this section, medical expenses are indeed massive.

Because so many shooting victims do not have health insurance, hospitals lose millions of dollars every year to treat them. The Violence Policy Center has noted that nonfatal gunshot wounds are the leading cause of uninsured hospital stays.[7]

The cost of treating gunshot wounds is compounded by the dramatic rise in the power of semiautomatic weapons used in crime. This has had a profound effect on the nation's emergency departments. Seldom do shooting victims just have one bullet wound. Furthermore, the velocity of the bullets packs an ever-increasing destructive force, causing more extensive damage to soft tissue and internal organs. This means that doctors are unable to save as many lives, and those who do survive experience greater, longer-lasting harm. The victims with multiple wounds almost always live more difficult and costly lives. This is especially true for spinal cord and brain injuries.

In working with filmmaker David Barnhart in the production of the documentary *Trigger: The Ripple Effects of Gun Violence*, I spent an entire morning at a hospital in Washington, D.C., speaking with a support group of men confined to wheelchairs for the rest of their lives because of gunshot wounds.[8] These paraplegics, whose ages ranged between twenty and fifty, are sobering, vivid examples of the collateral damage of living with mountains of guns. Trust me: they can never be described as "happy-go-lucky" or "carefree." The medical staff informed us that each person's medical costs would be at least $1 million per year for as long as they lived.

So who picks up the tab? Not surprisingly, the medical costs of firearm violence are borne by taxpayers and patients at the hospital who have health insurance. Hospital fee structures are adjusted regularly for insured patients, which help compensate for the hospital's losses in the expensive treatment of gunshot victims. And we often wonder how our medical care can be so expensive.

In chapter 9, we'll look at how doctors and nurses are becoming active in the movement against gun violence. And even though these medical costs are outrageously expensive, they are still not the biggest economic cost of the gun violence that plagues our country.

Security

Another segment of the financial costs of gun violence is security. To start unpacking what that means to the U.S. economy, start with city, county, state, and federal police forces. Be sure to add in private guards at gated communities, factories, skating rinks, and bowling alleys. You see security personnel every day. Perhaps you have been detained by them. Then think of millions more security personnel at public and government buildings, schools, hospitals, ports and airports, train stations, subways, banks, shopping malls, hotels, stores, and athletic facilities. We even hire security personnel at the retirement community where I live. With a mass shooting occurring almost every day now, more and more churches are hiring guards to be watchful while the preachers proclaim the gospel of love and God's peace that passes all understanding. Congregations may like to claim they trust in God, but more and more churches, synagogues, mosques, and other religious facilities are hiring security personnel. Just what does that mean in America?

Countless schools, sports venues, and theaters are purchasing metal detectors. The security business is thriving, and factories that manufacture scanners, alarm systems, and a host of other safety devices are reaping large profits. Meanwhile, the American taxpayer foots an enormous bill. Violence is so common it dictates the inclusion of expensive line items in most public and private budgets.

In 2009, the city of Chicago conducted a study of the annual cost of gun violence to the municipality. The answer was $2.5 billion, or $2,500 per Chicago household.[9] That's just one city. Consider the math for the country![10] But security still isn't the biggest economic cost of gun violence.

Criminal justice

The greatest economic collateral damage from guns and gun violence is found in the criminal justice system, including court costs and incarceration. In 1982, one in seventy-seven adults was in the correctional or judicial system in one form or another, totaling 2.2 million people. In just two decades, an explosive growth of both prisoners and others associated with the correctional system swelled its population to more than 7.3 million. Today, one in every thirty-one U.S. adults is connected to our criminal justice system.[11]

America's prison population has soared over the past quarter century. With only 5 percent of the world's population, the United States houses 25 percent of the world's prison inmates.[12] China, with a population four times larger than that of the United States, has roughly a quarter fewer prisoners.[13] Who pays the bills to keep these thousands of people behind bars? Who pays the billions of dollars for the construction of the most expensive architecture there is, and who foots the bill to keep our jails and correctional facilities operating to house those who break our laws? I'll give you one guess.

What is often called the school-to-prison pipeline funnels youth from disadvantaged schools straight into the criminal justice system. Thanks to zero-tolerance disciplinary practices and an increased role of law enforcement in schools, many students of color are being pushed into the court system. An African American friend remarked, "Our people are moving from underfunded schools to overcrowded prisons. If our country spent more dollars on schools and supplies for our underserved children, we would not need so many expensive

jails." This is a national disgrace. But what has caused this monumental rise in our prison population?

The culprit is the War on Drugs, which many have thought
would be the answer to fixing our high crime rates. But these
hopeful plans turned into a national disaster. We will address
this further in the next chapter.

Sensitive spirits should be asking many probing questions
about our expanding prison system. Why are we as a nation so
enamored with fighting crime, even minor crime, by punishing
people "to the fullest extent of the law"? Punishment seems to
be part of our American DNA. We always come back to "law
and order," which suggests a penal solution for every deviation.
When I was in college, my professors spoke of prisons as places
where offenders could "pay their debt to society" and be re-
habilitated in order to lead meaningful and productive lives.
Today we demand more severe penalties for offenders, even
though that approach leads to greater recidivism.

When our political leaders contend with one another about
who can be the toughest on crime and criminals, and wage an
"all-out war on drugs," or threaten our national adversaries
with destruction, seldom do we see the expected outcomes we
anticipated. Being tough and talking tough doesn't seem to actually *work*. What really works is an interdisciplinary approach
that focuses on restorative justice, which leads to healthier
solutions.

While attending an interdisciplinary conference in Boston,
I saw what was working in their city. Boston's civic leaders col-
laborate with families in stopping truancy, gang activity, and
violence before it becomes a pattern in young lives. They have
what they call "Operation Home Front," a program in which
police and clergy team up to walk the streets, meet neighbors,
and build trust in city neighborhoods. They visit homes of

youth at risk for gang involvement or detrimental behavior. Schools initiate these visits when a serious incident takes place or when problems at the school may negatively affect school safety. This initiative provides a crucial link for parents, students, and teachers to gain leverage in preventing social problems. The city's police force has earned a positive reputation for engaging with kids and building relationships and trust with the youth. Officers are frequently reminded that the police department can't "arrest its way to a peaceful city." Rather, peace requires human interaction, human compassion, and human cooperation.[14]

In chapter 10 we will look at the Ban the Box campaign and other effective approaches that will surely lower recidivism in urban America.

I wonder why people are so impressed with being tough and staying with approaches that just don't work. In the late 1960s, the renowned psychiatrist Karl Menninger published *The Crime of Punishment*, which discusses America's seeming need to punish others. One of Menninger's major emphases was to distinguish between punishment and penalty. "I think offenders should be penalized promptly and appropriately, but they should not be crushed, smashed, tortured, demoralized, and dehumanized," he wrote in a follow-up article about the book. "Punishment itself is a crime in two senses. First, it defeats its purpose—the control and reduction of crime. Second, it is a crime because it is inhumane, cruel, and soul-destroying. It doesn't make anything better for anyone. We are all its victims."[15]

Menninger summed up his book with a clear call for change: "Until the general public can replace sheer fear and anger and vindictiveness with intelligent planning and wholehearted cooperation with the police, the wardens, the judges and other public servants, the incidence of crime will not greatly diminish."[16]

The NRA and gundamentalists heartily disagree. One of their consistent messages is that gun violence prevention is futile. For them, the proverb "An ounce of prevention is worth a pound of cure" is null and void. The only solution to crime, they say, is punishment. In their minds, prevention also smacks of "gun control," which they regard as a draconian measure. They affirm that the only thing that works is the threat of severe punishment, to the fullest extent of the law.

It's ironic how prevention seems to work in other significant areas of our lives. We diligently get vaccinations to prevent polio, hepatitis, tetanus, measles, and other diseases from ravaging our bodies. We go to doctors and dentists for annual checkups to prevent more serious problems from arising. We schedule automobiles, trucks, buses, and airplanes for routine maintenance that prevents disastrous mechanical breakdowns. When we don't prevent problems, the results can be disastrous. Deferring preventive maintenance in older buildings, for example—especially in mechanical and electrical systems—frequently turns minor problems into major system failures.

Nevertheless, the corporate gun lobby has convinced Congress and state legislatures that gun violence prevention does not work. This ensures that the collateral damage to the infrastructure of our society will be enormous. Refusing to prevent the violence *we know will take place* in certain communities and relying on punishment to fix our problems is worse than closing the barn door after the horse is gone.

Every election cycle, lawmakers who bemoan "runaway spending" in our federal and state budgets need to take a long look at the $229 billion annual price tag that gun violence exacts—a price shouldered by taxpayers. The passage of reasonable gun laws, which would not impinge on anyone's gun rights, would dramatically lessen these exorbitant costs.

8

WHOSE LAW AND ORDER?
The Interface of Guns, Racism, and Poverty

J EMEL ROBERSON WAS twenty-six years old and the father of a little boy. He was a well-loved musician and often played keyboard and drums for local churches and participated frequently in community gatherings. Roberson's dream was to become a police officer, but to provide for his family, he was working as a security guard at a bar in the Chicago suburbs. In the early morning hours of November 18, 2018, there was a fight in the bar and gunshots rang out. Roberson, who was Black, drew his gun and detained the subject. When the police arrived, a white officer mistook Roberson for the suspect, even though he was wearing his security uniform, and opened fire, killing Roberson.[1]

Days later, on Thanksgiving, Emantic Bradford Jr., age twenty-one, was shopping at a mall in Alabama. Bradford was a caretaker for his father, a former correctional officer who had cancer. He had a concealed carry license. Police were called to the mall where an active shooter had been reported. Bradford, who was Black, pulled his gun to protect other shoppers. This is exactly what gun rights advocates would say he should have done. When police arrived, they saw a Black man holding a gun. They killed Bradford with three shots to the back. The officer who shot him was not charged.[2]

Roberson and Bradford were truly what the NRA's Wayne LaPierre would call "good guys with guns." They both owned their guns legally, carried them on their person, and they both used them to try to protect others. They were exactly what the NRA says we need more of: good guys with guns in public spaces. They could have served as NRA poster boys, but the NRA has been silent about these murders. Both men ended up dead because the cops shot first and asked questions later.

We cannot talk about guns without talking about race. Gun violence cannot be isolated from the violence of racial injustice, white supremacy, discrimination, and bigotry. In this chapter we look at how racism is connected to gun violence, often in more complicated ways than white observers claim or are ready to admit.

It is essential that those of us who are white realize how insidious and powerfully subtle these maladies really are. The virus of white supremacy lives within us; we don't have to be aware of it for it to exist. Racial injustice is a slow violence, often enacted in what seems like slow motion, over generations, but cloaked with niceties. But racism is not entirely disconnected from the swifter violence of guns, as we will see. To dismantle both the violence of racism and the collateral damage caused by mountains of guns, we must understand how we came to this moment in time.

For sixty years as a Presbyterian minister, I preached often on the themes of justice and compassion, taught hundreds of classes, and marched in demonstrations for peace and justice. For forty-five years I have devoted my energies to preventing gun violence. Yet only in the last few years have I realized the extent to which my *semi-hidden feelings of white supremacy*—rooted in the systematic, structural advantaging of white people based on a belief that they are superior to people of color—has harmed millions of Black people and other people of color. It is painful for me to take an honest, critical look at my social and spiritual blindness. But I only have a few years left, and I want to leave this earth having played a small part in helping to dismantle racial injustice and bigotry instead of silently resigning myself to it. I recommend a similar journey to all who benefit from white privilege and white supremacy. But, first of all, we must look at how we got here in the first place.

"Life must be lived forward, but it can only be understood backward" is a common paraphrase of the words of Danish theologian Søren Kierkegaard. Similarly, the late Myrtle Brock, a history teacher in Jones County, North Carolina, understood that the past is prologue, and wisely counseled, "To know nothing of the past is to understand little of the present and to have no conception of the future."[3] Understanding how forty thousand people die at the barrels of guns each year, and grasping why tens of thousands of Black and brown people are incarcerated for years in for-profit prisons for committing minor crimes, and figuring out why being Black apparently disqualifies one from being a "good guy with a gun"—these realities require serious reckoning with the past. This chapter's examination of the history of racial injustice in the United States is brief, and I commend to you several books that plumb the depths: *The Cross and the Lynching Tree* by James H. Cone, *The New Jim Crow* by Michelle Alexander, *Stamped from the Beginning* by Ibram X. Kendi, *Rethinking Incarceration* by Dominique

DuBois Gilliard, *Trouble I've Seen* by Drew G. I. Hart; *Blood Done Sign My Name* by Timothy B. Tyson, and *The Warmth of Other Suns* by Isabel Wilkerson.

Can God's people admit there are dots to connect between our violent past, our racist domination and penal systems, and our current trust in guns? If we can honestly repent, then and only then is there hope for building the beloved community for which Martin Luther King Jr. gave his life. In that beloved community, we discover what the apostle Paul called "a still more excellent way" of love (1 Corinthians 12:31).

From slavery to Jim Crow to Vietnam

While this part of the book will focus on the experience of Black people, we cannot forget that the Indigenous peoples of America were the first to experience racism and domination by white Europeans. Figuratively speaking, all Native Americans were forced to walk "the trail of tears." They were enslaved and displaced. Their cultures came within an eyelash of being erased. The Doctrine of Discovery, first promulgated by Pope Nicholas V, gave white Christian nations "moral and legal rights to invade and seize Indigenous lands and dominate Indigenous Peoples" in America and all over the world. Under the guise of bringing Christianity to people the world over, the doctrine simultaneously decimated their cultures and replaced them with European cultures and ideals. The third president of the United States, Thomas Jefferson, endorsed the doctrine. The patterns of oppression stemming from the Doctrine of Discovery live on in papal bulls, royal charters, and U.S. Supreme Court rulings "as recent as 2005."[4]

America's racism grew uglier with the introduction of slavery. Resistance from enslaved people, the Underground Railroad, the moral crusades launched by abolitionists, and the Civil War ended the brutality of slavery. No longer could white men and women buy or sell other human beings and pretend they were their property. It was no longer socially acceptable to *own* another human being. Slavery's demise, however, simply gave way to another kind of systemic discrimination against Black people. What is commonly known as Jim Crow was a structured system that classified people with darker skin as inferior human beings. The framers of the Constitution had helped perpetuate the scam by declaring years earlier that the representative value of enslaved people was three-fifths that of free whites. Jim Crow doctrine tried to hide the bigotry of segregation behind the more mannerly phrase "separate but equal." That so-called nicety guaranteed the separation of the races and simultaneously imposed countless hardships and indignities that kept people of color from quality education, political enfranchisement, and socioeconomic advancement and opportunity.

Among the humiliations and discrimination that Black people had to endure were rock-bottom wages; inferior, poorly equipped schools; separate waiting rooms in bus and train stations; separate sections in movie theaters; separate toilets and drinking fountains. Paved roads literally stopped at the borders of Black neighborhoods, amusement parks were off-limits, and water and sewer lines did not extend into their neighborhoods.

Fast-forward to World War II, in which over one million African Americans served in the military.[5] During the war, they received but a few honors and privileges, but after the war it was back to business as usual, and they were expected to live under Jim Crow. One of the more egregious forms of discrimination for a nation that prides itself on "freedom and justice for all" was systematically depriving Black veterans the benefits of the G.I. Bill.

To express the nation's gratitude for their military service, veterans were given the opportunity to sign up for the G.I. Bill. Members of my family took advantage of it and received free college educations, paid for by a grateful nation. The G.I. Bill also provided generous bank loans that enabled veterans— mind you, *white* ones—to buy a house, raise a family, and start living the American dream. The G.I. Bill helped sixteen million veterans "attend college, receive job training, start businesses and purchase their first homes." Years later, President Clinton praised the G.I. Bill as "the best deal ever made by Uncle Sam . . . [which] helped to unleash a prosperity never before known."[6]

But Black veterans received significantly less help than their white counterparts. The program was administered in such a way that "thousands of black veterans in the South—and the North as well—were denied housing and business loans, as well as admission to whites-only colleges and universities." They were excluded from certain types of job training and were directed toward lower-paying jobs and smaller Black colleges "which were pitifully underfinanced and ill equipped to meet the needs of a surging enrollment of returning soldiers."[7] "The law was deliberately designed to accommodate Jim Crow," writes Ira Katznelson in *When Affirmative Action Was White*.[8] Such calloused injustice bears its poisonous fruit to this day.

Living on the "right side of the tracks" in the 1960s as a white preacher in a southern town, I hardly noticed the poverty in which my African American neighbors were forced to live. I did preach regularly about God's love for all, and how justice demanded that we put an end to segregation and treat all people as equal members of God's human family. I took some criticism for my sermons and received a few threatening phone calls. But I was still unable to really *feel and understand* how my whiteness was "money in the bank" for me, but kept my Black brothers and sisters from climbing the socioeconomic ladder.

Just one example of the heartlessness of Jim Crow in my community occurred when an African American man had a heart attack at his home and died. The local funeral home operated an ambulance for emergency use for the community. But as a matter of so-called principle, it could not be used to transport a Black man to the hospital fifteen miles away. It just wasn't "proper."

In 1954, the Supreme Court decision in *Brown v. Board of Education* signaled an end to "separate but equal" schools. Especially in the South, whites felt that integration and racial equality was being forced upon their way of life, and that they were not getting the respect they were due. Five southern state legislatures passed fifty new Jim Crow laws; the Ku Klux Klan reasserted itself and performed castrations, lynchings, and bombings of Black citizens' homes and churches.[9] One cannot understand the history of America without grasping the horrors of the lynching tree, as theologian James Cone reminds us so eloquently in *The Cross and the Lynching Tree*. "To forget this atrocity leaves us with a fraudulent perspective of this society and the meaning of the Christian gospel for this nation," Cone writes.[10]

Are white perpetrators of domination and injustice able to learn from those who were systematically oppressed? Gurdon Brewster, a white Episcopal seminary student in New York City, spent the summer of 1961 with "Daddy King," the father of Martin Luther King Jr., as civil rights struggles heated up across the Southland. In his book, *No Turning Back: My Summer with Daddy King*, he writes about some of what he learned in that turbulent summer. It is a must-read for anyone who seeks to understand how we got here. In a chapter entitled "Singing

Hymns," Brewster tells of visiting an elderly, blind African American woman who always sang from her depths. "Always wondered what white folk sing about," she said to him one time, almost talking to herself. She continued,

> "No slavery, can't sing about freedom. No hunger, can't sing about the Lord's banquet. Never driven from your home, can't sing about the Promised Land. Never had no cross burning in your yard, no lynchings in your family; can't sing about deliverance. Always wondered what white folks sing about. I guess when you're on top there's no place to go but down. They sing about bein' across the river on the other shore." Her voice dropped off into a nearly inaudible whisper. "But they left some of us behind. How do you sing about that?"[11]

From "law and order" to the War on Drugs

After the assassinations of Malcom X, Martin Luther King, and Robert Kennedy, there were riots and outbreaks of crime in major cities. The nation was on edge. In 1968, a Gallup poll revealed that 81 percent of all Americans agreed with the statement that "law and order has broken down in this country," and most of those polled blamed African Americans and the Communists, "who started the race riots." [12]

Presidential candidate Richard Nixon saw not only a window but a door of opportunity and scheduled seventeen speeches on law and order for his election campaign. He bought television ads featuring frightful music, accompanied with images of protesters, bloodied victims, and fierce-looking Black men in proximity to gun violence. At the close of one ad a voice intoned Nixon's promise: "I pledge to you, we shall have law and order in the United States."[13]

The beginning of a new system was on its way. The language of "law and order," by itself, appeared to many to be devoid of any racial assumptions. But Black activists and others soon discovered the specifics, and after reading the small print, they began to shout, "*Whose* law and *whose* order?"[14]

The emphasis on law and order turned out to be disastrous for Black people, especially in cities. The details of "law and order" would end up supporting the ghettoization of Black and brown people. At the same time, we watched thousands of our brightest and best young people, of all races, come home in body bags. The bags did not distinguish between the races. The Vietnam War was dividing the nation. Shootings and violence were reported in every newspaper; crime, drugs, and gangs were rampant; factories that previously made shotguns and rifles for hunting and recreational shooting retooled and began selling handguns and military-style weapons for civilians to buy for personal protection. The citizens of the strongest nation in the whole world were inordinately afraid. Law and order captured the imaginations of white citizens, and encouraged them to fight crime both at home and on the other side of the globe to stop the spread of godless communism so America could "keep the world safe for democracy."

According to Nixon's former domestic policy advisor, John Ehrlichman, the War on Drugs became a political tool to fight Nixon's enemies: "the antiwar left and black people." Decades later, in an interview with Dan Baum of *Harper's* magazine, Ehrlichman confessed to the administration's sophisticated dirty tricks. "We knew we couldn't make it illegal to be either against the war or blacks, but by getting the public to associate the hippies with marijuana and blacks with heroin, and then criminalizing both heavily, we could disrupt those communities. We could arrest their leaders, raid their homes, break up their meetings, and vilify them night after night on the evening news. Did we know we were lying about the drugs? Of course we did."[15]

Thus "law and order" morphed quickly into the War on Drugs, which has been operative since the 1960s, thanks to Presidents Nixon and Reagan, with an assist from President Clinton. The War on Drugs was conceived with great fanfare and gave hope to many Americans, even to some Black people who supported the "race-neutral" concept. But the details of the plan would be devastating for Black and brown people in urban America for years to come. Our cities and national economy are still reeling from these knee-jerk, racist attempts to fix our drug and crime problems by blaming them on the poorest members of our society. Through the rationale provided by the War on Drugs, authorities were able to throw thousands of people of color into prison for what were minor crimes, branding them for life as felons.

President Nixon signed the Controlled Substances Act (CSA) into law in 1970, declaring that drug abuse was "public enemy number one." According to a 1969 Gallup poll, about 48 percent of Americans thought drugs were a serious problem, particularly in underresourced neighborhoods of America's largest cities. Nixon's initiative increased federal funding for drug-control agencies and imposed strict mandatory prison sentences for drug crimes. He also created the Drug Enforcement Administration (DEA) in 1973, which was responsible for tackling drug use and smuggling in the United States.[16]

The War on Drugs had a hiatus during Jimmy Carter's presidency, but it returned with a vengeance under President Reagan. Under Nixon, the War on Drugs was something like war games. But under Reagan, the War on Drugs was a blitzkrieg. From 1981 to 1989, Reagan doubled down on Nixon's policies, reinforcing and expanding them. He teamed up with his wife, Nancy, who launched the "Just say no" campaign, an effort to educate children on the dangers of drug use. The whole country fell in with McGruff the Crime Dog and vowed to get tough on crime.

What all these efforts really created was "the criminalization of poverty," under which the poorest Americans went to prison for minor drug offenses and petty nonviolent crimes, while the same crimes in white communities were ignored or the offenders given the proverbial slap on the wrist. Reagan's emphasis on drugs led to a colossal increase in incarcerations for nonviolent drug crimes. President Clinton continued the expansion of the prison system. Legal scholar Michelle Alexander, citing the work of sociologist Loïc Wacquant, writes, "During Clinton's tenure, funding for public housing was slashed by $17 billion (a reduction of 61 percent) in order to boost the construction of correctional facilities by $19 billion (an increase of 171 percent), 'effectively making the construction of prisons the nation's main housing program for the urban poor.'"[17]

Mass incarceration can be better explained by changed policies about crime than by crime rates themselves.[18] In 1986, Congress passed the Anti-Drug Abuse Act, which established mandatory minimum prison sentences and eliminated judicial discretion for drug offenses, thus increasing the prison population. The law was later disparaged for its racist ramifications, particularly as it allocated longer prison sentences for offenses involving the same amount of crack cocaine as offenses involving powder cocaine. The chemical composition of these two substances is nearly identical, but crack cocaine could be sold in smaller doses at lower prices. As early as the 1980s, over 90 percent of convicted crack offenders were Black, and 5 percent were white. Powder cocaine offenders, however, were predominantly white. Drug users in communities of color were, and still are, often viewed as offenders committing crimes worthy of incarceration, while white users are most frequently seen as victims in need of treatment and rehabilitation. As Alexander notes, "People of all colors *use and sell* illegal drugs at remarkably similar rates." In fact, she continues, "If there are significant differences in the surveys to be found, they frequently suggest that whites, particularly white youth, are more likely to engage in drug crime than people of color."[19]

Data show that people of color have been targeted and arrested on suspicion of drug use at much higher rates than whites, leading to disproportionate incarceration rates. Urban neighborhoods lost large numbers of people to incarceration, which actually increased incentives to sell drugs—most notably crack cocaine—which, in turn, led to a spike in gun purchases and more violence.

Thus, in less than thirty years, the U.S. penal population exploded from around three hundred thousand to more than two million people, "with drug convictions accounting for the majority of the increase. The United States now has the highest rate of incarceration in the world, dwarfing the rates of nearly every developed nation and even surpassing those in highly repressive regimes like Russia, China, and Iran. In Germany, for example, 93 people for every 100,000 adults and children are in prison. In the United States, the rate is roughly eight times that, or 750 per 100,000."[20]

According to the Pew Research Center,

> The racial and ethnic makeup of U.S. prisons continues to look substantially different from the demographics of the country as a whole. In 2016, blacks represented 12% of the U.S. adult population but 33% of the sentenced prison population. Whites accounted for 64% of adults but 30% of prisoners. And while Hispanics represented 16% of the adult population, they accounted for 23% of inmates. Another way of considering racial and ethnic

differences in the nation's prison population is by looking at the imprisonment *rate*, which tallies the number of prisoners per 100,000 people. In 2016, there were 1,608 black prisoners for every 100,000 black adults—more than five times the imprisonment rate for whites (274 per 100,000) and nearly double the rate for Hispanics (856 per 100,000).[21]

The United States cannot continue to blame and imprison people of color for our social crises of crime, drugs, gangs, and guns. We cannot arrest our way to peaceful cities by throwing the most vulnerable citizens into prison for nonviolent crimes. Both morally and economically, our nation cannot afford policies that force Black and brown people who have paid their debt to society to live the rest of their lives bearing the stigma of being labeled a felon, which is, in reality, almost a death sentence (more on this later in this chapter and in chapter 10). With the label "felon," one can't find a good job or even receive food stamps to keep body and soul together.

Mass incarceration and who benefits

In her landmark book, Michelle Alexander calls mass incarceration the New Jim Crow: a "new system of racialized social control [that] purports to be colorblind . . . [and] operates in a tightly networked system of laws, policies, customs, and institutions that operate collectively to ensure the subordinate status of a group defined largely by race."[22]

Were there other ways we could have responded to the national drug crisis? Some countries, like the Netherlands, faced with rising drug crime and troublesome rates of drug abuse and addiction, chose to respond with medical treatment, prevention, education, and economic investment in crime-ridden communities. Portugal decriminalized possession of all drugs and provides treatment to those who are addicted. In the United

States our leaders chose to punish offenders to the fullest extent of the law, and so we built more private prisons. Meanwhile, Dutch and Portuguese officials watched the numbers of those addicted to hard drugs decline by half. Ten years later, drug-related crime had declined dramatically in both countries.[23]

Unfortunately, America was once again committed to "getting tough on crime." We blamed and punished the disenfranchised and manipulated the poor. Full-blown arrests for minor offenses such as driving with expired license plates, broken taillights, not coming to a full stop at stop signs, and possession of small amounts of marijuana became the norm for law enforcement. Meanwhile, political leaders portrayed those arrested as the opponents of law and order. They just *happened* to be Black. The New Jim Crow was in full swing. "More African American adults are under correctional control today—in prison or jail, on probation or parole, or awaiting trial—than were enslaved in 1850, a decade before the Civil War began," writes Alexander. "The mass incarceration of people of color is a big part of the reason that a black child born today is less likely to be raised by both parents than a black child born during slavery.[24]

Thousands of Black men and women have been warehoused into prisons and jails, locked away for drug crimes that are largely ignored when committed by whites. A particularly insidious part of the War on Drugs is how the DEA and law enforcement agencies were given extraordinary powers to legally profile and make arrests by race and send those arrested to prison. Legal scholar David Cole has exposed these profiling practices, which are so expansive that they "potentially [justify] stopping anybody and everybody" on a hunch.[25] As Alexander writes,

> The profile can include traveling with luggage, traveling without luggage, driving an expensive car, driving a car that needs

repairs, driving with out-of-state license plates, driving a rental car, driving with "mismatched occupants," acting too calm, acting too nervous, dressing casually, wearing expensive clothing or jewelry, being one of the first to deplane, being one of the last to deplane, deplaning in the middle, paying for a ticket in cash, using large-denomination currency, using small-denomination currency, traveling alone, traveling with a companion, and so on. . . . The Florida Highway Patrol Drug Courier Profile cautioned troopers to be suspicious of "scrupulous obedience to traffic laws."[26]

Is it any wonder that many African Americans have a jaded view of police and America's justice system? Too many have been arrested for "driving while Black," and irresponsible members of law enforcement have claimed the right to humiliate the driver with a spread-eagle search while colleagues scour the car looking for small amounts of marijuana and an excuse to put another person in jail. Even today, this is SOP (standard operating procedure) in many large cities.

As James Cone writes, it is appalling that "nearly one-third of black men between the ages of eighteen and twenty-eight are in prisons, jails, on parole, or waiting for their court date. Nearly one-half of the more than two million people in prisons are black. That is one million black people behind bars."[27] Who benefits from that?

Furthermore, despite their sustained presence in prisons and jails, "the voices of black women are often excluded from discussions about the criminal justice and corrections systems," writes criminal justice professor Breea Willingham. "Mainstream ideas about prisons are usually those of men, and any references to women in prison are usually those of white women."[28] Willingham cites the work of Victoria Law, who helped start Books through Bars, a group that sends free books to people in prison throughout the country. "The stereotype of the male felon makes invisible the growing number of women imprisoned under the various mandatory sentencing laws passed within the past few decades," writes Law. "Because women do not fit the media stereotype, the public does not see them."[29]

Dying small towns and cities across the land are encouraged to consider erecting for-profit prisons to revive their local economies. Private prison contracts often require the government to keep on funneling people into the system, even if actual crime rates are falling. According to reporter Michael Cohen, "nearly two-thirds of private prison contracts mandate that state and local governments maintain a certain occupancy rate—usually 90 percent—or require taxpayers to pay for empty beds."[30]

Even before the Trump administration's daily invective against immigrants began, the Immigration and Customs Enforcement's detention budget included a congressional mandate that at least thirty-four thousand immigrants be detained on a daily basis. This quota has grown each year. "Private prisons have profited handsomely from that policy," writes Cohen, as they own nine of the ten largest ICE detention centers.[31]

The pay-for-prison lobby is, in effect, selling human bodies to an industry for shameful profit. This privatization "created the atmosphere that made the 'Kids for Cash' scandal possible, in which two Pennsylvania judges received $2.6 million in kickbacks from for-profit juvenile detention centers" for sending more than five thousand kids to their facilities over a five-year span. The children received "unusually long sentences."[32]

Who else stands to profit from mass incarceration? First, each arrest by law enforcement nets a given city or county $153 in state and federal funds.[33] Consider the bail bond companies that collect $1.4 billion in fees from defendants and their families. The fees are nonrefundable. The industry also "actively works to block reforms that threaten its profits, even if reforms could prevent people from being detained in jail because of their poverty." In addition, "specialized phone companies" garner monopoly contracts and charge families who want to keep in touch with their loved ones up to $24.95 for a fifteen-minute phone call. There is also the modern equivalent of "the company store." Commissary vendors sell goods at inflated prices to those who are incarcerated—"people who rely largely on money sent by loved ones." These sales bring in $1.6 million a year.[34]

When men and women are pulled from a community and put in the criminal justice system in alarmingly high numbers, mostly for minor drug offenses, we are taking away fathers, mothers, brothers and sisters, uncles and aunts, and cousins. Families are broken up, and the poor get even poorer. According to the president of the Safer Foundation, a nonprofit that supports people with criminal records, if the family's breadwinner is in jail, the family's income drops 22 percent. "And when they come back home," he said, "they will earn 40 percent less for the rest of their lives because they have a record."[35] This enacts a major blow to an entire neighborhood.

After people serve time, having "paid their debt to society," they return to their impoverished neighborhood with a new identity they must carry for the rest of their lives. They are felons, no matter how minimal the offense. The label "felon" never goes away. All the old forms of discrimination that keep people poor and nonproductive automatically come into operation at the mention of the word. As Michelle Alexander points out, "Today it is perfectly legal to discriminate against criminals in nearly all the ways that it was once legal to discriminate against African Americans. Once you're labeled a felon, the old forms of discrimination—employment discrimination, housing discrimination, denial of the right to vote, denial of educational opportunity, denial of food stamps and other public benefits, and exclusion from public service—are suddenly legal." In fact, Alexander says, once you are labeled a felon, "you have scarcely more rights, and arguably less respect, than a black man living in Alabama at the height of Jim Crow."[36]

Alexander's point is critical, and one that we cannot ignore. As Alexander writes, "We have not ended racial caste in America; we have merely redesigned it."[37]

Guns and racism

Parks and playgrounds, good schools, recreational facilities, grocery stores with bountiful supplies of fresh fruits and vegetables, after-school and summer opportunities for youth, medical and dental facilities for all, consistent trash collection, and safe streets: these things are common in many sections of our cities but not in the poorest neighborhoods. Residents in many urban neighborhoods simply do not have the resources to live the American dream. Very few have good jobs with benefits. Most make less than the minimum wage and frequently work two jobs. Employers save lots of money by hiring workers for fewer than forty hours a week, thereby avoiding overtime pay and having to provide healthcare, parental leave, and vacation time, which usually start with forty-hour-a-week employment.

The median Black household has a take-home income that is about half that of white households. Families of color will soon make up the majority of the population, but most continue to fall behind whites in building wealth. As *Forbes* reports, "The median white household will own 86 times more wealth than its Black counterpart, and 68 times more wealth than its Latino one."[38]

Furthermore, underserved neighborhoods are not simply a "byproduct of the modern city," something that just happens and no one seems to know why. Such areas are a "'prime moneymaker' for those who profit from land scarcity, racial segregation, and deferred maintenance."[39] A pastor friend who has a church in the inner city informed me that 70–80 percent of people's wages in underserved neighborhoods go to landlords for rent. Should excessive complaints surface about inadequate facilities, renters' belongings are put out on the curb, and the cost of relocating is prohibitive. It's best to just bear with a less-than-perfect residence. The fact is, most of the residents cannot just pick up and move to a better neighborhood. Racism and discrimination keep them stuck without good schools or jobs that pay a living wage. In this desperate situation where everything seems to be stacked against them, people may look to guns to provide a measure of stability and protection. They are cheap, plentiful, and easily accessible. You can even rent one for a day.

What about the kids? Residents often pool meager resources or alternate giving childcare to the children in the community, but too many children are left to fend for themselves. Where do they turn to keep body and soul together? At least in a gang they have a sense of belonging and respect. Firearms come to be regarded as access to power and resources, as well as protection, and unfortunately, too many gang members feel like a gun makes them "real men." Socioeconomic marginalization, particularly the collapse of good educational structures, undermines a community's ability to exert social control. The City of Los Angeles interviewed many male gang members, who spoke to "the absence of their fathers and lack of attention from positive father figures and role models as a central deficit in their lives."[40] Mass incarceration stands at the center of that reality.

Indeed, when you sense that your community is under siege, and when jobs that pay a living wage are hard to find and systemic racism hinders opportunities, guns can lend a sense of safety and power that is otherwise inaccessible.

When my friend Alonzo Johnson started his first pastorate in Philadelphia, he was on his way to a Boy Scout celebration in his church when he met two parishioners in the hallway. The two women were discussing guns. He joined them for a few moments and one of them asked, "You have a gun, don't you, Preacher? Everybody has a gun in Philadelphia." Alonzo replied, "No I don't have a gun. I have an alarm at my house." Her reply revealed much: "Not everybody can afford an alarm."

In the conversation, Rev. Johnson learned it would be difficult to convince many of his parishioners that a gun in the home was more of a risk than a source of power and protection. The residents believed their guns guarded what little power they had.

Gun violence in America's cities is a problem of monumental proportions. About 60 percent of firearm homicides take place in the poorest neighborhoods of America's largest cities. The psychological, economic, and spiritual costs of this violence to neighborhoods alone are staggering, but the collateral damage of the carnage affects every single American. Martin Luther King Jr. was right when he observed, echoing the words of Emma Lazarus, that none of us is free till all of us are free.

In 2010, the rate of firearm homicides for Blacks was 14.6 per 100,000, compared to 2.7 for Native Americans and Native Alaskans, 1.9 for whites, and 1.0 for Asians and Pacific Islanders.[41] Many politicians regard gun violence in the "inner city" as a crime problem, but for white suburban communities, gun violence is regarded more as a public health issue.[42]

Shootings in urban communities of color receive much less media attention than shootings that occur in mostly white or more affluent communities. America has seldom seen the flurry

of news reports, TV coverage, and public grief over the tragedy of Sandy Hook, where twenty first graders were callously
gunned down. Of course, it was well publicized, *and it should
have been*. Yet in that same week, there were at least a dozen
gun homicides in Chicago, Detroit, Baltimore, and St. Louis
that received only a smattering of attention. There was more
news coverage of Sandy Hook than for the 260 schoolchildren
who were killed in Chicago between 2007 and 2010. A sizable
number of social critics agree that the media ignore urban
shootings in which most of the victims range in age from their
early teens to mid-twenties, and in which victims are Black or
brown. It is no secret the media gravitate to mass shootings, just
as they do to the spectacular anywhere.

The tragedy of the Parkland high school shooting in Florida
in February 2018 gave many students who survived the motivation to build a national response to gun violence. In June
2018, several of them traveled to Chicago to meet high school
students who had also lost friends and peers in shootings. They
understood one another immediately and quickly bonded.
Fifteen-year-old Lauren Hogg of Parkland and sixteen-year-old
Kaiseona Lockhart of Chicago walked the streets together. "We
don't need to say anything," said Hogg. "We all understand the
pain." Gun violence happens daily in Lockhart's neighborhood.
"We all experience trauma," she said. "Out here, you become
immune to it." The Chicago teenagers, wrote a reporter for the
Washington Post, "have grown tired of hearing outsiders catego-
rize the gun violence on their streets as a gang problem, which
they say allows lawmakers to avoid confronting a more nuanced
reality." They expressed hope that the presence of Parkland students would help in exposing "other factors linked to the violence, such as unemployment and failing schools." The visit was
an eye-opener for David Hogg, age eighteen, who has become a

national spokesperson for common-sense firearms legislation. "Until his activism he never realized how violence in neglected black and Hispanic neighborhoods are judged differently than violence in majority white communities like Parkland."[43]

"The way we talk about incidents of gun violence in this country—and the solutions we propose to stem future acts of violence—seems to be dramatically different depending on the race of those involved," writes Joshua Horwitz, executive director of the Coalition to Stop Gun Violence. To make his point, he tells of the sad death of twenty-five-year-old Kajienne Powell in St. Louis in 2014. Powell, who was Black, stole two drinks and a pastry from a local convenience store, but made no attempt to escape. "Instead," writes Howell, "he placed the cans on the ground and paced nervously back and forth. When two police officers arrived on the scene, he walked toward them holding a kitchen knife, yelling, 'Shoot me!' As he closed in on the officers, they obliged, shooting him dead."[44]

It was a classic case of suicide by cop. Yet very little of the national discussion about the incident mentioned mental health, which was undoubtedly part of the situation. "Instead," Howell writes, "we got the standard character assassination that is so common when African-Americans are involved as perpetrators." Howell invites us to consider the comment made by NBC contributor Jeff Halevy: "Knife-wielding thug just robbed a store. Get over it. It's not always race."[45]

But when mass gun violence involves a white perpetrator (Howell cites people such as Jared Loughner, James Holmes, and Elliot Rodger), "the conversation *immediately* turns to mental health. The shooter was 'deranged' and probably on medication, we are told." And we hear accompanying comments like "He seemed like such a nice person" and "No one in the neighborhood saw this coming."[46]

After the not-guilty verdict in the 2012 George Zimmerman case, in which Zimmerman, who identifies as Hispanic, was acquitted in the shooting death of Trayvon Martin, a Black teenager, the Black Lives Matter movement was born. Maya Angelou, one of our nation's most celebrated poets, expanded in our minds the numbers of those who were devastated by the tragedy. She said:

> A number of people think that only blacks were hurt by this decision, but that is not true. All you have to do is look at the protesters—they are white and black, Spanish-speaking and Asian. What is really injured—bruised, if you will—is the psyche of our national population. We are all harmed. We are all belittled, and we give to the rest of the world more ammunition to sneer at us. . . . It really makes me see how far we have to go, that one man armed with a gun can actually profile a young man because he is black and end up shooting him dead. It is so painful.[47]

Horwitz writes, "We cannot look away [from the gun violence in urban America] and still maintain our humanity. We have to keep our eyes wide open and face the agonizing reality of all the lives destroyed by guns—not just the ones that grab the media's attention. The high-profile deaths are tragic, but gun violence goes well beyond the headlines. We must recognize that every life lost to gun violence is a national disgrace. Everyday gun violence is a stain on this country that can only be cleansed by action. The names of the fallen—all of them— are our motivation to act quickly. Let's get to work!"[48]

From cowardly to brave conversations

We have so much work to do. We have so many conversations ahead. Race can be difficult for white people, especially, to talk about. Eric Holder, former attorney general of the United

States, once said, "Though this nation has proudly thought of itself as an ethnic melting pot, in things racial we have always been and continue to be, in too many ways, essentially *a nation of cowards*. . . . It is an issue we have never been at ease with and given our nation's history this is in some ways understandable. And yet, if we are to make progress in this area, we must feel comfortable enough with one another, and tolerant enough of each other, to have frank conversations about the racial matters that continue to divide us."[49]

As a white man, I know how difficult these conversations can be. Not all of us are ready to admit that being white carries enormous privileges. The word *privilege* comes from the old French and basically means "a right, advantage, favor, or immunity granted to a certain individual, group or class, and withheld from certain others or all others." White privilege is something like a "private law."[50] I look upon white privilege as the unspoken assumption that my whiteness somehow makes me more worthy of trust from the general public, department store clerks, civic authorities, educators, law enforcement, and others than that afforded to people of color. I've never been followed by clerks in department stores who suspected that I might be a shoplifter. Barack Obama, former president of the United States, is unable to make such a statement. I've never been arrested for "driving while white," but my Black friends are well aware police use racial profiling to arrest them for minor traffic infractions. People of color, particularly young Black men, know very well they can be arrested for driving with a broken taillight and even shot and killed, as was Walter Scott in Charleston, South Carolina, in 2015.[51] At the opening of this chapter we read of two Black men who were trying to protect others, but were shot and killed by police.

Jamilah Pitts, a high school teacher and a Black woman, writes that her students of color are themselves afraid to say the word *white*, or to discuss the source of "the blatant racism of slavery and Jim Crow." She continues, "If that is the case, imagine how much more difficult it is for them to engage in dialogue about mass incarceration rates; the militarism of police; the killing of innocent black men and women; cycles of poverty; the destruction of our bodies, minds, and souls; and gentrification. These are all symptoms of a type of racism that remains deadly to this day because, despite bodies lying in the street, we refuse to talk about it."[52]

Pitts puts the onus for breaking the silence and having these difficult dialogues squarely in the laps of teachers—we must also include clergy—and offers concrete and creative ways to begin. Teachers, pastors, and other leaders can start with the admission that we are also scared, frustrated, angry, guilty, confused, hurt, or uncomfortable. Pitts follows her comments with excellent suggestions for teachers on how to have honest conversation. She writes, "Teaching as an act of resistance and teaching as an act of healing are not mutually exclusive."[53]

So how do we begin to find healing? How do we resist the powers of the corporate gun lobby and offer alternatives and hope? Perhaps holy resistance begins with exposing truths to light. The most significant and loving action that Christians can take is to shine the light of gospel truth on the myths and misinformation surrounding the meaning of guns in our society.

9

COME TO THE LIGHT
Exposing Falsehoods, Advocating for Truth

TRANSPARENCY IS NOT a word that gundamentalists champion. The corporate gun lobby works hard to keep the public uninformed about the nature and extent of the collateral damage caused by guns. Yet as we move toward solutions to what can only be called a crisis in our civic life, transparency is exactly what we need. We need research, facts, transparency, and truth.

The National Academy of Sciences recently identified the pressing need for up-to-date, accurate information on how many guns there are in the United States, their distribution and types, how many people acquire them, and how they are used. As we will see in this chapter, the NRA and Congress responded to the scientists' pleas by mandating national ignorance. They dread scientific research and public knowledge about what is happening today with America's 393 million guns.

I'm reminded of those little critters that live under rocks and hate the light. As a child, I liked to watch those creepy-crawly bugs scurry about after I picked up a rock and exposed them to the sunlight. Perhaps that is why I titled my first book *America and Its Guns: A Theological Exposé*. As Christians, we are called to walk in the light of Christ. Light has a way of exposing secrets in the corners, and of illuminating lies that masquerade as truth. Jesus reminded us, "All who do evil hate the light and do not come to the light, so that their deeds may not be exposed. But those who do what is true come to the light, so that it may be clearly seen that their deeds have been done in God" (John 3:20-21 NRSV).

In this chapter we shed light on some of the deepest commitments of the corporate gun lobby, which include keeping the public in the dark about the true extent of the crisis. To reduce the collateral damage of gun violence, we need light, and a lot of it. We begin by shining the light on a myth that still captivates most of us—a myth that we must expose if we are to move forward.

Myth of redemptive violence

In this book we've focused on domestic gun violence. We've said little about our nation's armaments, which can obliterate entire cities with sophisticated missiles fired from submarines under the sea or by drones guided to their targets from thousands of miles away. But national military policies and domestic gun violence are, in many ways, two sides of the same coin. Both reveal our national faith in the values and effectiveness of violence. It's hard to say which comes first. Does our national commitment to buying excessive amounts of weaponry for the military stem from our fascination with efficient guns that can fire a hundred rounds a minute and shoot through the walls of our homes? Or do 393 million guns seem necessary because we are proud to be the most powerful fighting force in the world? It is a chicken-and-egg kind of question, but each of these modes of violence is controlled by the same animating spirit that says, "Violence is what works. It may not have worked every time in the past, but it is really going to work *this* time."

We may put "In God we trust" on our money, but given our 393 million domestic guns and the largest military in the world, our ultimate trust appears to be in our weapons and the violence they project. I always carry a little chart in my wallet about how much America spends on its military compared with other powerful nations in the world. Unfortunately, my chart is always out of date. It just can't keep up with the increases. My 2017 chart shows base expenditures of $523.9 billion, while the 2018 figure jumps to $574.5 billion.[1] Military spending is the second largest item in the U.S. federal budget, second only to Social Security. We spend more on defense than *the next eight countries combined*—that is, China, Saudi Arabia, Russia, the United Kingdom, France, India, Japan, and Germany.[2]

I have loved editorial cartoons ever since I was in high school. They speak in compelling ways about current events and the capricious human spirit, and I frequently find them more persuasive than the most eloquent editorials. One of my all-time favorite cartoons shows a king standing at the base of a high wall. He is surrounded by his generals, all bedecked with medals and ribbons. At the base of the wall are the scattered remains of Humpty Dumpty. The king speaks: "Yes, I know all the king's horses and all the king's men cannot put Humpty Dumpty together again, but Humpty's death should tell you why I need fifty thousand more horses and one hundred thousand more men."

People in the United States tend to think there are two kinds of violence: 1) the despicable violence of our adversaries, whether real or imagined, and 2) the redemptive violence we must be ready to use to defend our loved ones or our American values. Theologian Walter Wink says that the myth of redemptive violence refers to a violence that pretends to save. This myth enables us to act as if the violence that we are forced, by circumstance, to use is redemptive, while the violence used by our enemies is utterly deplorable and perpetrated by madmen. "From the earliest age children are awash in depictions of violence as the ultimate solution in human conflicts," writes Wink. The myth of redemptive violence, he says, "is the simplest, laziest, most exciting, uncomplicated, irrational, and primitive depiction of evil the world has even known."[3]

Trusting in redemptive violence carries with it enormous collateral damage. It costs us domestically, on average, forty thousand lives a year, devastated families, and the erosion of the common good. In the name of "God-given gun rights," we witness not only the loss of precious lives but the steady decimation of our human values, the erosion of our democracy, and an increasing contempt for international law and institutions such as the United Nations. All the above perpetuate an exploitive society in which, as Wayne LaPierre of the NRA likes to say, "The guys with the guns make the rules."[4]

LaPierre's statement may be truer—and sadder—than he realizes. In a democracy, elected officials, chosen by voters, make the rules. But when people with guns create such a strong lobby that they effectively buy the silence and complicity of government officials, evidence, research, and facts become casualties, and democracy dies in the dark.

Ban on federal funding for research

In 1996, the Centers for Disease Control and Prevention spoke favorably about the possibility of approaching gun violence as a public health issue. The NRA and the corporate gun lobby immediately pounced, accusing the agency of promoting gun control. As a result, Congress went to work to strip away the agency's funding. *The Dickey Amendment,* introduced after the NRA lobbied Congress to ban all federal funding for public health research on gun violence, mandates that none of the funds made available for injury prevention and control at the CDC be used "to advocate or promote gun control."

Interestingly enough, before his death, Jay Dickey, the representative from Arkansas who introduced the amendment, asked his former colleagues to *repeal* the legislation he had introduced. He acknowledged the need for systematic research. Why do so many legislators discover the "right thing to do" only after they leave office?

A case in point is President Ronald Reagan, a proud member of the NRA. Journalist Francis Clines writes that Reagan was a hero of the gun lobby for "steadfastly maintaining his opposition to handgun control even after he was critically wounded in a 1981 assassination attempt that left a bullet 'an inch from my heart,' as he noted." After recovery, basking in the adoration he received from gun enthusiasts, Reagan called for the abolition of the Bureau of Alcohol, Tobacco, and Firearms, which enforces federal gun safety laws. But two years after he left office, Reagan "surprised the nation by endorsing the Brady Law that established federal background checks of firearm buyers for criminal records and histories of mental disturbance." He confessed that his support for the law was inspired by Jim Brady, his press secretary, who had been partially paralyzed by a gunshot wound from the assassination attempt. In an op-ed for the *New*

York Times, Regan wrote that "this nightmare might never have happened" had the Brady Law been in effect. Thanks in part to Reagan's support, the law was eventually passed in 1993.[5]

Reagan then joined former presidents Jimmy Carter and Gerald Ford in endorsing the 1994 assault weapons ban. The measure, which banned a range of military-style guns and large-capacity ammunition clips, narrowly passed. Proponents credited Reagan's support for their victory. Just imagine how many lives would have been saved had Reagan endorsed sensible gun laws while he occupied the Oval Office.

After the Dickey Amendment passed, the CDC installed a self-imposed ban on direct research. That action dried up their funding, which "had a chilling effect felt far beyond the agency: Almost no one wanted to pay for gun violence studies. . . . Young academics were warned that engaging in research was a good way to kill their careers."[6] Thus a small minority of gun zealots and their cronies in Congress, subsidized by gun and ammunition manufacturers, is browbeating the entire scientific community and telling them what aspects of our culture they can and cannot study.

After several mass shootings, President Obama in January 2013 ordered the CDC to once again study "the causes of gun violence." Still they did not budge. They were afraid of the risks. Congress, furthermore, continued to block direct funding.[7] Since the mid-1990s, there has been no research on particular firearms laws, policies, or aspects of gun violence to measure their effectiveness in reducing crime or gun deaths.

Advocates argue convincingly that "efforts to suppress gun research have resulted in more lives lost." They point to other public health research, like studies on motor vehicle deaths and studies on smoking, which saved lives without banning cars or cigarettes. Public health advocates are convinced they can do the same for gun safety and do it "without infringing on the rights of law-abiding gun owners."[8]

The national debate today about gun control isn't about "what would work or which policies would actually stop or reduce gun violence." Instead, it has become a one-sided discussion on what can pass Congress. As reporter Dylan Scott writes, there is no clearer sign of "our collective psychosis around the issue of gun control [than that] proposals are reverse-engineered from political feasibility. . . . To make matters worse, Congress perpetuates a status quo that makes it difficult for researchers to even begin to quantify which policies would actually lead to fewer Americans dying violent deaths."[9]

Daniel Webster, a researcher at Johns Hopkins University, believes Congress is "bottling up" data because of pressure from the NRA. "There's scant research on underground gun markets and how they differ in places where gun laws are relatively strict versus places with pretty lax laws," he said. His colleague Cassandra Carifasi added that, given the lack of data on nonlethal shootings, "we only have the tip of the iceberg of gun violence in this country. We have more and more people dying and experiencing injuries from gun violence every year, and we're still having problems getting basic research done because we can't get the data or the fundings."[10]

Between 1996 and 2012, CDC research funding for gun violence fell by 96 percent, according to Every Town for Gun Safety. "Major public research funding for gun violence prevention is estimated at $2 million annually," the organization reports. "By contrast, in 2011, the National Institutes of Health devoted $21 million to the study of headaches."[11]

"There'd be a lot more research if there was money," says David Hemenway, a Harvard University epidemiologist. More research would result in better ideas for reducing gun violence.

Thus, lives continue to be lost as these prohibitions "lead to a vicious cycle in which gun rights activists use the lack of strong evidence for gun control against any proposals that would restrict access to guns."[12] Steven Novella, a professor at Yale Medical School, writes that those in opposition face the "paralysis caused by insufficient information." All of this, he says, means that the corporate gun lobby can oppose "any gun legislation by arguing there isn't evidence proving the legislation will work. If that standard were used for all legislation across the board we would have a very different style of government in our country."[13]

Gun rights hardliners have typically waved away the need for more research as they retreat to their old saws. To reduce gun violence, they say, we need to make sure all criminals are prosecuted and punished; we don't need any more studies or any more laws. "The public doesn't need to know" is the mantra. It's hard to imagine a more destructive one.

Creating and then neutering the ATF

The 1970s were a tumultuous time in America. The debacle of Vietnam, ongoing civil rights struggles, riots and unrest in urban areas: these episodes inspired enterprising gun enthusiasts to take advantage of a tremendous financial opportunity. They began retooling the factories that turned out rifles and shotguns for hunting and recreational purposes and started manufacturing the handguns that a fearful public was demanding for self-defense. Many of these handguns were made on the cheap and did not include safety mechanisms. Others were made of such inferior steel that a leading gun magazine warned that a particular gun was not accurate "beyond nostril range" and should not be on the market.

Even so, Congress had to deal with this huge increase in private handgun sales, which required, according to the Second

COME TO THE LIGHT / 149

Amendment, some kind of regulation. In 1952, the Alcohol and Tobacco Tax Division (ATTD) of the IRS was formed. With the passage of the Omnibus Crime Control and Safe Streets Act of 1968, as well as the Gun Control Act of 1968, federal firearms legislation was overhauled, and the scope of the agency expanded. These laws also empowered the ATTD to enforce laws against the criminal use of explosives.

In 1968, the division was renamed the Alcohol, Tobacco and Firearms Division (ATFD) of the IRS. In 1972, Congress established the Bureau of Alcohol, Tobacco, and Firearms (ATF), whose mission was to oversee the manufacture, distribution, sale, and possession of firearms in America. But further decisions had to be made about the oversight of guns in America. The Congress really had two options for the new agency. ATF could oversee a *well-regulated* militia, the course defined by the Constitution, or it could oversee a *poorly regulated* militia, the course coveted by those who manufactured, distributed, and sold firearms to the public. Congress chose the latter.

Even a casual study of the regulations that govern ATF's general oversight of guns in America reveals it is intentionally made weak and ineffective at doing the job for which it was created. Just a few reasonable laws to keep guns out of the hands of dangerous people would save thousands of lives, but such laws would inevitably stop several gun sales and that would hurt the bottom line of the multibillion-dollar gun industry. Congress chose to keep the ATF under its thumb by enacting a series of absurd laws that perpetuate murder and mayhem throughout the country. In short, our gun laws are designed to protect the sales of guns and make it more difficult for law enforcement to stop illegal or "questionable" sales.

Consider, first of all, the agency itself. From its beginnings, it has been grossly understaffed. The ATF began work in 1972 with twenty-five hundred agents charged with inspecting all the gun dealers in the United States. These inspections "are meant to ensure, among other things, that [gun dealers] keep complete sales records so guns used in crimes are traceable, and that they don't sell their wares to those forbidden to buy them. However, those inspections are few and far between."[14]

Even though America's guns and dealers have multiplied many times over since 1972, the number of agents working for the ATF today remains at 2,500. Their job description has not changed. To put that meager number of agents in perspective: the New York City Police Department has more than 34,000 uniformed officers who patrol New York's streets, and 51,000 employees overall.[15] But while the responsibilities of those 34,000 officers end at New York's city limits, the responsibilities of ATF's 2,500 agents to oversee the business of guns in America extend from coast to coast.

According to a 2013 Office of the Inspector General report, less than 60 percent of firearms dealers were inspected within five years. According to a McClatchy article, "In 2016, ATF inspected just 7.1 percent of 137,464 active firearms dealers for compliance. At that rate, it would take the agency 14 years to inspect all firearms dealers—likely longer, as the number of dealers is steadily increasing."[16] Today the United States has more gun dealers than McDonald's, Starbucks, and supermarkets combined. There are fifty thousand more gun stores than McDonald's restaurants.[17]

The ATF's goal to inspect each dealer every three to five years is unfulfilled. (Notably, the goal used to be every three years but was relaxed to allow for inspections up to every five years.) Yet the gun lobby has taken measures to ensure that these inspectors don't become a nuisance to gun sellers. The ATF is legally barred from inspecting a dealer more than once a year without a special warrant.[18]

These disclosures are not to disparage the goodwill and commitments of the dedicated staff of the ATF. With very limited resources and an impossible job description, they rein in the most unscrupulous gun dealers. Research demonstrates that a tiny fraction of gun dealers are responsible for most of the guns found at crime scenes throughout the country.

ATF officials know exactly who the rogue dealers are. Yet because of a law passed by Congress in 2003, they're not permitted to share that information with the general public. "As a result, solutions for stanching the flow of guns from these dealers to crime scenes remain frustratingly out of reach," not only for public health researchers but for the ATF itself.[19]

These bad-apple dealers engage in gun trafficking, accept straw purchases, hire nefarious personnel, and "lose" thousands of guns out their back doors every year. The ATF does the best it can to subtly expose them to the general public, but the law is the law and does not permit transparent disclosure. For dedicated agents, it must be like going to work every day with one hand tied behind your back.

It's absurd that the corporate gun lobby fights to the death any and all regulations and restrictions on guns themselves. But those entrusted to maintain the integrity of gun commerce in the country have restriction after restriction placed on them and their work so they will not interfere with gun commerce.

Below are ten of the many regulations and limitations under which the ATF must work on a daily basis:

1. The Gun Control Act of 1968 gives the ATF authority to check gun dealers from coast to coast for illegal sales, but only once every twelve months.

2. The identities of U.S. dealers who sold guns seized at Mexican crime scenes are to be removed from public view.

3. The AFT has the power to revoke licenses under certain conditions, but the "fire sale loophole" enables corrupt gun dealers who have lost their licenses to sell their remaining inventory without imposing background checks on any purchasers. Congress has introduced legislation to close this loophole, but it has yet to pass.[20]

4. Licensed gun dealers must keep specific records of firearms sales, but the ATF cannot use those records to compile a database of gun owners.

5. In 2003, Congress passed a law that bars federal law enforcement from releasing any information to the public that links guns used in crimes to the original purchaser or owner. These names are reported only to state and national databases for prohibited purchasers.[21]

6. More than seven thousand guns are stolen from cars and thirty thousand per year are stolen from licensed gun dealers, but the ATF's plea that dealers perform an annual audit was voted down by Congress.[22]

7. The Consumer Protection Act of 1972 prohibits the Consumer Protection Commission from examining the quality or safety of *any* gun or piece of ammunition. Teddy bears, dolls, and toy pistols have vigorous safety standards. Real guns are off-limits.

8. According to a 2000 report, over 50 percent of guns taken from crime scenes come from only 1 percent of gun dealers, but the ATF is blocked from disclosing their activities or intentionally putting them out of business.[23] (While the ATF says it no longer uses that study to evaluate current crime trends, there is no more-recent data, in part because the ATF is prohibited from sharing gun tracing information with the public.[24])

9. When a dealer *does* go out of business, the dealer is required to send all their records to the National Tracing Center

in Martinsburg, West Virginia. Police and law enforcement agencies throughout the country regularly ask the center for information, but the center's employees cannot readily access it. In 2009 there were twelve thousand boxes stacked up to the ceiling in its facilities waiting to be copied *by hand* because the center is prohibited from using computers for a significant part of their work, including gun control matters.[25]

10. The 2010 Appropriations Bill for major law enforcement agencies reveals the limits Congress imposes on the ATF. For the FBI there are nineteen lines of congressional direction; for the DEA there are ten; for ATF there are eighty-seven, "including the requirement to *keep the gun-tracing database hidden from the public.*"[26]

The above are only a few of the gun laws that bring colossal collateral damage to everybody in America.[27] The NRA is indebted to a public which asks them and the puppets who follow their lead in Congress very few embarrassing questions about such farcical gun laws.

If a gun shop in your area is engaged in the lucrative illegal business of trafficking, shouldn't you as a citizen have a right to know about that? It's strange that the very law enforcement agency commissioned to investigate illegality is *by law* required to be so tight-lipped about its work.

In the future, when the NRA or politicians rail against the tyranny of big government, remind them that facts matter, and it is inconceivable that the public continue to be kept in the dark about the crime that plagues our communities and the guns that perpetuate it.

Follow the money

At the time of this writing, Congress is having a national gun control debate sparked by the shooting in Parkland, Florida.

Well, that's what the media say. Yes, our elected officials have talked some about guns, but their conversation is a sham. Their exchange has not been about what policies would stop or reduce gun violence. It has been a one-sided, partisan caucus on what can actually pass Congress, which is under the thumb of right-wing gun rights ideologues.

Republicans are traditionally opposed to any and all regulations, especially when they pertain to making guns more difficult to obtain or use. In the long run, these measures cost many human lives. If Americans are committed to saving lives and preventing gun violence, we must change the minds of committed Republican legislators. Republicans may be as dismayed as Democrats by our national gun pandemic, but when it is time to vote, they consistently support the corporate gun lobby that hates any regulation of its killing machines and wants Americans to buy more firearms.

Aren't forty thousand gun deaths per year and $229 billion in economic costs sufficient reasons to vote for a few reasonable laws that do not infringe on anyone's gun rights? Why don't these obscene numbers translate into votes that have the support of 90 percent of the American people, including gun owners? What other issue is so systematically blockaded? What keeps these lawmakers in lockstep with the billion-dollar gun industry?

When something appears so nonsensical, we often say, "Follow the money." And there is hard evidence that the NRA and the larger gun lobby donate millions of dollars every year to lawmakers of both political parties who follow their bidding. The vast majority of these contributions, however, end up in the coffers of Republican legislators. The corporate gun lobby can bank (no pun intended) on solid Republican votes so the industry can keep on selling guns.

Linking the gun lobby with the Republican Party is not to disparage a valued political party. I was born and raised in its tent, and I love my many family members who are Republicans. I am simply stating the obvious. Let's be honest. In addition to the money trail that unites the NRA with the Republican Party, they have a common enemy: big government. Every election cycle we hear from Republican gundamentalists that the federal government wants to flex its muscles and confiscate all of America's 393 million guns and remove Second Amendment rights. The not-so-subtle suggestion is, "If they are coming for our guns, the government will make off with our other rights and freedoms as well." (This testimony is usually followed by some reference to the hundreds of thousands of servicepeople who spilled their blood to protect our freedoms.) Their mantra has become "Vote freedom first." Many Democratic legislators have also bought into their paranoia and also received "A" ratings from the NRA—along with nice campaign checks—but it is common knowledge that the corporate gun lobby prefers Republicans.

While we all cherish our freedoms, when "freedom" becomes a shibboleth (as in "Vote freedom first"), it loses its essential meaning as well as its power. The German writer Johann Wolfgang van Goethe reminds us: "None are more hopelessly enslaved than those who falsely believe they are free." *Second Amendment, Constitution*, and *gun rights* are also very effective code words, at least in the state where I live. In truth, they often render reason null and void. If we listen to NRA and gundamentalist fears, we are led to believe that freedom, the Second Amendment, the Constitution, and gun rights are in grave danger and the rights of all Americans could go down the tubes. That is not so. Not one of these cherished American concepts is in any danger whatsoever. We need to encourage our Republican family members and friends to listen not to the rhetoric of a tiny cadre of gun extremists but to the reasoned voice of former president Ronald Reagan, who supported universal background checks and a ban on assault weapons.

It's not common that advocates of reasonable gun policy hear good news from our legislators, be they Republican or Democrat, but I have good news. This comes from Joshua Horwitz, executive director of the Coalition to Stop Gun Violence: "In 2013, the Consortium for Risk-Based Firearm Policy developed the extreme risk law. This law allows family members and law enforcement to petition a court to temporarily remove guns from individuals at risk of harm to self or others. Six years later, 14 states and the District of Columbia have passed this law, and dozens of other states have plans to introduce the legislation. Among those 14 states, 5 Republican governors affirmatively signed these bills into law. And these new laws are saving lives."[28]

As we go to the polls, I pray that God will say once again to us all, "Come now, let us reason together, . . . though your sins are like scarlet, they shall be as white as snow; though they are red like crimson, they shall become like wool. If you are willing and obedient, you shall eat the good of the land; but if you refuse and rebel, you shall be devoured by the sword" (Isaiah 1:18-20). Brothers and sisters, God does not want us devoured by swords or by firearms.

This *is* our lane

Few professionals are as acquainted with the collateral damage of gun violence as our physicians. Thankfully, when it comes to our absurd gun laws or inane understandings of gun rights, America's doctors are not rolling over and playing dead. They are speaking out loudly and clearly and demanding action.

They are shedding light on the falsehoods under which we are trying to live. Because "no good deed goes unpunished" in this crazy world, the Florida branch of the NRA recently sued physicians, particularly psychiatrists and pediatricians, for asking depressed patients or the parents of curious children if there was a gun in the house. The NRA's argument was that asking about a gun in the home is not a medical question but a political one, and one that disparages gun owners and constitutes political harassment. The Eleventh Circuit Court of Appeals sided with the doctors, who were not to be muzzled.[29]

With recent upticks in gun violence and mass shootings, the NRA is making the same argument again. They were angry about a 2018 position paper from the American College of Physicians that called for a public health approach to firearms-related violence and the prevention of firearms injuries and deaths. The paper declared the medical profession has a "special responsibility" to speak about the prevention of such injuries and to support, among other measures, "appropriate regulation of the purchase of legal firearms."[30]

In an angry tweet, the NRA mocked physicians and urged them to stick to medicine. The tweet scolded "self-important anti-gun doctors" and directed them to "stay in their lane" and not get involved in the gun debate. Dr. Judy Melinek, a forensic pathologist, was angry about the tweet but didn't know quite how to respond. Two days later, as she was on her way to the morgue to examine the body of one of the country's many forgotten gunshot victims, the words came to her. "Do you have any idea how many bullets I pull out of corpses weekly?" she tweeted. "This isn't just my lane. It's my [expletive] highway."[31] Many in the medical community, who must try to repair the results of violence on a daily basis, launched a hashtag to share their perspectives: #ThisIsOurLane.[32]

"We aren't against the second amendment," Melinek told *The Guardian* newspaper:

> What we are against is not researching, not putting effort into researching, and not putting the funding into researching what can be used to prevent gun violence and death, whether it's trigger locks, security, training or the idea of requiring insurance and having people have insurance in case their gun is used to kill someone else. We need to have the research and we need to have the data to back it up, and right now that's not happening. We need to do something, and telling doctors to stay in their own lane is not the way to do it. We're the ones who have to deal with the consequences. We're the ones who have to testify in court about the wounds. We're the ones who have to talk to the family members. It breaks my heart, and it's just another day in America.[33]

If we could, by some benevolent fiat, declare gun violence a public health issue and treat it as such, we would be well on our way to a more peaceful nation. We would watch gun deaths decrease. The approach for a public health matter is not to cast blame on any individual or group of individuals. Public health interests itself in specific measures that would save lives. Yet for decades, the NRA and its co-conspirators have turned heaven and earth to stop any suggestion that gun violence might become a public health issue—even as our modern killing machines wipe out tens of thousands every year.

So what can we do? What can churches and individual followers of Jesus do to heal our land and reduce the bewildering numbers of people harmed by gun violence?

10

SHOW LOVE, DEMAND JUSTICE
Some Modest Proposals for Change

MPATHY, CARE, AND COMPASSION for neighbors are the most visible indicators that we believe in a caring God. In Jesus' parable of the good Samaritan in Luke 10, the man showed neighborly love to a total stranger who had fallen among thieves and was left on the road to die. We are surrounded today by neighbors who appear in a million guises and are left on our roads to breathe their last. Jesus' parable teaches us that our neighbors are always worthy of our attention, our time, and our money. Actual victims of gun violence have been left on the road to die. And we've seen throughout this book that the rest of us suffer with untold collateral damage brought by so many guns.

The statistics can be numbing and the news reports overwhelming. After reading a book like this, you may feel paralyzed by despair, fury, or grief. What can we do as churches and as individual Christians? In the parable of the good Samaritan, before the Samaritan loved the victim, two very religious people refused to love him. The questions for today's church include,

How can we truly *see* the countless victims of gun violence and love them? And how can we work to prevent more deaths and injuries from guns in the future?

If you want to learn what love really means, stay away from Hallmark greeting cards. They will overwhelm you with schmaltzy sentimentalism and oceans of emotions, which are often given as the very reasons why one is unable to love—that is, "I didn't feel like it." Love is not warm, fuzzy feelings or sweet sentimentality. If you want to learn of love, go to the Bible and meet the action verbs that tell you what love really is. "Sweet love language" is much less common in the New Testament than one would expect, and the verb forms of the word *love* are mentioned with far greater frequency than the nouns. Love is active and engaged.

I was amazed to realize recently that in the synoptic gospels—Matthew, Mark, and Luke—Jesus rarely says, "God loves." Instead, Jesus says things like: God cares for his creatures and clothes the grass and feeds the birds. God makes the sun rise on the evil and the good. God sends rain on the just and the unjust. God does not forget the lowly sparrow. God numbers even the very hairs of your head and mine. God forgives and is patient with all his people's sins. God agonizes over and searches for those who are lost. God heals. God saves. God feeds. God rebukes demons. God tells people of their infinite worth. And God in Christ put a cross on his back and lugged it up a hill. God in Christ was nailed to it, suffered, thirsted, bled, and died for us all. Love, says the New Testament, is a verb. Love may be a lot of things, but it is first and foremost the most practical, sensible, and effective act in the world.

In Matthew 25, love translates into food and drink, a warm welcome, clothes, ministering to the sick, and visits for the prisoner. John's gospel does speak often in the language of love, and

I'm glad it does. But in every instance except one, John uses the Greek word *agapē*. That word always refers to the giving away of one's self and one's own prerogatives to meet the needs of another, whether they are physical, mental, or spiritual. Agape means laying down one's life for another. Jesus says in John's gospel that if we love him, we will love all our brothers and sisters, for we belong to the same human family.

What follows are specific, practical deeds of agape love. These are ideas for living out your desire to demonstrate concern for those who are caught up in the web of gun violence. Loving God and loving our neighbors in our gun-saturated culture means tangible acts like these.

Study the issue and invite others to join you

When you hear your television spew out the gory details of the next mass shooting, or when you learn of a person killing his wife and children before turning the gun on himself, or when you discover that a dear friend has committed suicide, you may cry and pray. Those are in order. Yet it is not enough for you to weep and say, "Isn't that terrible!" It is not enough to lament, "Why doesn't somebody *do* something?" It is not enough even to say a prayer and then get back to business as usual. That is *not* enough. You can and must do more.

You can help stop the madness by educating yourself about the stranglehold that guns have on our culture. As you begin to understand how we got to this point in the United States, you will learn how to separate fact from fiction, lies from truth. You can begin taking action to heal our broken communities. It must start with education. As you discover that the gun laws Congress writes today do not protect our people but rather those who manufacture the guns and ammunition, you are on your way to being a change agent. When you have factual information and data at your fingertips, you can bear witness to the truth. As Antisthenes, an ancient Greek philosopher, is said to have written, "The most useful piece of learning in life is to *unlearn* what is untrue." What are you waiting for?

I'm not bashful to recommend the three books I have written to educate the faith community on what we can do to build peaceful communities. Take a look at *America and Its Guns: A Theological Exposé* (2012), *Gundamentalism and Where It Is Taking America* (2017), and the book you are holding now. Recruit a reading partner. Read a chapter in any of these books or others of a similar nature and then discuss it. If your church or faith community is not already studying the issue, get some friends and go to your pastor or governing body. Inform them you want to start a study group or Sunday school class. Trust me: there are lots of people who share your concerns.

Talk to friends, family members, and acquaintances who believe guns protect us and make our communities safe

Perhaps in the past you have had hurried discussions about America's guns with people on the street, at a ball game, or after a civic club meeting. It's less likely you have had an in-depth discussion with people with whom you disagree on this topic.

Bend over backward to show love and respect for those with whom you disagree about guns. Provide a friendly setting— invite people into your home to have an honest discussion with individuals or a small group. Because I have never met a meal I didn't like, I encourage you to have some pizza or a bowl of chili together. Assure your guests that although you may come at the subject from different places, you believe it is important to share mutual concerns, and that you promise a civil discussion. Wouldn't it be a blessing to gather friends to rationally discuss two constitutional values: the right to keep and bear arms and a commitment to the general welfare and domestic tranquility? If you want some guidance on starting such a conversation, the organization Living Room Conversations (LivingRoomConversations.org) provides helpful information.

You want to make it a learning experience for all parties. Another approach may be to share books with one another that best describe your stance, and use those writings to begin an honest discussion. Such discussions can be difficult, but they are crucial for healing to happen in our gun culture.

Educate your neighbors

Another powerful act of love is to educate your neighbors about the risks of having a gun in the home. Reputable data from lengthy studies indicate that for every incident in which a gun in the home is used in self-defense or in a legally justified shooting, there are "four unintentional shootings, seven criminal assaults or homicides, and eleven attempted or completed suicides."[1]

Maybe there should be a law requiring every gun dealer to place a conspicuous sign at their front door that reads "Those most likely to harm or kill you are your family members and friends." That would cut into their profits. The FBI's Uniform Crime Reports prove this reality year after year. The greatest threats to life and limb are *not* strangers, foreigners, terrorists, immigrants, criminals, or people of a race different from your own—the groups that the corporate gun lobby wants us to fear so we will depend on guns for safety. The most dangerous persons to our lives and limbs likely live on our block. That is the plain, unvarnished truth, but it is a very difficult truth for most people to comprehend. The gun industry cannot sell the numbers of guns it wants to sell by telling customers their own family, friends, and neighbors are the ones most likely to harm them.

Don't be afraid to ask if there are guns in the home

This is addressed to parents, grandparents, and caregivers: You must realize that significant numbers of gun owners do not lock up their guns when they are not in use.

Here is a story from one of my colleagues who worked for the Million Mom March, Carole Price. One day in 1998 she told her twelve-year-old son John that he could go to their neighbors' house. John never came back. His friend's father had recently purchased a new gun to protect the family and had stored it—loaded—in a dresser drawer. John's friend wanted to show it to his buddy. In the process, he accidentally shot John.

Remember how these tragedies play out. Remember that in that incident John was not the only victim, even though he is the only one who would show up in statistics. Remember John's parents, friends, and classmates, and particularly never forget John's good friend. He will live with the knowledge that he killed his friend. This is lifelong collateral damage. Carole frequently tells people: "If you think asking a neighbor if they have a gun in the house or if it is locked up is difficult—trust me, picking out your child's casket is much harder."

Understand the complexities of guns, racism, and poverty

We can't have an honest conversation about guns without acknowledging that African American communities are disproportionately affected by homicide. The Violence Policy Center notes, "For the year 2015, blacks represented 13 percent of the nation's population, yet accounted for 51 percent of all homicide victims. . . . For black victims of homicide, like all victims of homicide, guns—usually handguns—are far and away the number-one murder tool. Successful efforts to reduce America's black homicide toll, like America's homicide toll as a whole, must put a focus on reducing access and exposure to firearms."[2]

It is common knowledge that over 90 percent of an iceberg lies below the surface, unseen and invisible. What lies below the surface is what makes maneuvering in places where icebergs exist dangerous and even treacherous. Numerous studies have shown there is an undeniable relationship between racism, gun violence, and poverty. People may quickly ascertain that poverty and gun violence are intimately connected, but that is only the tip of the predicament. Many people don't talk much about the racism that lies below the surface of our social consciousness and interactions. But the racism inherent in our economic systems shapes the entire zip code where we live and who our neighbors are.

If our nation is to be just, we must spend considerable time trying to understand the complexities of economic and racial justice. As we saw in earlier chapters, the costs of racism and gun violence are huge: loss of employment opportunities, mass incarceration, broken families, hospitalization, trauma for family members, pain, post-traumatic stress. It's a much bigger problem than just gun deaths. But the issues of racially segregated communities and the underresourced and underfunded social welfare infrastructure must be addressed along with the carnage caused by guns.

We must not be shy to speak of poverty, mass incarceration, drugs, and exploitive violence. The conversation must involve *all of us*, not just a few of us. This may not be easy for white people who have lived for generations in dominant positions, but our collective future depends on honest dialogue and solidarity. If you have ever been in an uncomfortable conversation you wished you could avoid, you know it is possible to talk all around the subject and never get to the nitty-gritty. God wants us to go right to the nitty-gritty. Learn the facts. Understand the complexities. Only then can we move forward.

Listen to the marginalized and seek their guidance

It is imperative that all Americans talk about gun violence with one another, especially about the havoc it has wreaked in communities of color. In the following paragraphs I am speaking to white people and those whose communities have not been directly affected by gun violence. We must get up close and personal and listen to the pain of those who often hear gunshots before they go to sleep at night. We must show up in people's lives, even those we have never met, and together seek loving and practical responses. Above all, it means seeking the guidance of those who live in marginalized communities.

Before my wife and I went to Japan as missionaries in 1965, a significant change took place in the way mainline American churches regarded and recruited missionaries. Before World War II and shortly thereafter, churches overseas were struggling. There were few mechanisms in place to oversee the work of the white missionaries who heard God's call to work in their countries. In short, too many missionaries worked independently instead of collegially with local churches. They were responsible only to themselves and to their own mission group. They saw what they felt needed to be done and they usually did it—without asking for help or advice from local or national leaders.

In the late 1950s and early 1960s, by the grace of God, new understandings developed on what kind of missionary help, if any, should be put in place. National churches through the years had grown stronger, and these former "receiving churches" began inviting missionaries (who were usually white) to come and help them preach, teach, or perform a particular ministry. Former "mission lands," as we used to call them, were adamant they did not want or need the "old-time missionary who listened only to God." It became clear in every country where we "did mission work" that missionaries would no longer be independent from the oversight of the local or national church. They were expected to see themselves as invited guests and partners. They were not invited to "fix things" or have all the answers. Conversely, they were expected to discuss with their colleagues what needed to be done, but final decisions were determined by the local or country leaders.

Well-intentioned white people who go into marginalized communities can do a lot of harm. Showing up is important, but just as important is *how* we show up. Denise Anderson, former co-moderator of the Presbyterian Church (USA) and a friend of mine, tells it like it is. In a personal letter she counsels:

> White supremacy often leads white people to come to marginalized communities as well-meaning saviors, which tends to do more harm than good. A lot of white intervention is experienced as intrusive. Seeking the guidance of the marginalized should be done on the terms of the marginalized, not on the terms of those who decided one day to wake up and do something about racism, poverty or gun violence. Moreover, the problems in these neighborhoods won't immediately bend to white will (as most things do). It will take long-term engagement. So, if you're not in it for the long haul, stay home. The kinds of allies these communities need are those that respect their self-determination.

Whites and affluent communities that are relatively free of poverty and gun violence need honest partnerships with those who live in less privileged areas. After all, our faith wasn't born in a palace or the rich suburbs; it came to us from a stable. Its first announcement was made to peasants and outcast shepherds on a hillside. It was prepared in a carpenter's shop, and had its beginnings at the very bottom of the socioeconomic ladder. Our Lord teaches that all people, even the most vulnerable, are sacred to God. Jesus began at the bottom of the scale himself, identifying with the poor and outcasts, calling them his brothers and sisters. He commanded us to love them and, by the grace of God, together live in hope.

We must demonstrate by word and deed as well as by honest humility that every human being is precious. Each person is a somebody who deserves our love, our attention, our time, and our money. If this were not so, would almighty God have commanded us to love our neighbors as ourselves?

Call your representatives

Everyone who is concerned that one hundred or more people in the United States needlessly die at the barrels of guns every day should make it a personal priority to call their representatives regularly. Remind them that most of our citizens—including NRA members—support reasonable gun regulations.

For starters, see what the Coalition to Stop Gun Violence revealed in 2019 as its top five legislative priorities (below). Use your phone to raise your voice for justice and peace. It's easy. Dial 202-224-3121 and ask the operator to put you in touch with your congressperson or senator. Come on board and use your voice.[3]

Support universal background checks on every gun sold. Here is the truth: 92 percent of Americans—as almost every recent poll suggests—support universal background checks on all guns sold. Such a regulation would do away with the "gun show loophole," in which unlicensed sellers can attend any of the roughly five thousand gun and knife shows and sell *any* gun to *anyone* with no questions asked. Even NRA members support such a law. Universal background checks would also do away with straw purchases, which occur when a person who cannot pass a background check hires or persuades someone with no criminal record to buy a gun and pass it on. Straw purchases are a major source of crime guns in the country.

Advocate for extreme risk laws. Extreme risk laws allow individuals or police officers to ask a judge to temporarily remove guns from the possession of an individual deemed to be in crisis. "Using evidence-based criteria for dangerousness, extreme risk laws are able to identify individuals at a heightened risk of violence without unfairly stigmatizing those living with mental illness," writes Josh Horwitz, executive director of the Coalition to Stop Gun Violence. Eight states passed new extreme risk laws after the 2018 shooting at Marjorie Stoneman Douglas High School, bringing the total number of states with such laws to seventeen, while several more are considering such legislation.

Support an assault weapons ban. The ban on these weapons expired in 2004. Since then, Horwitz points out, mass shootings have become "more frequent and far more lethal." AK-47s and AR-15s and similar models that can shoot a hundred or more rounds in one minute are the weapons of choice for mass shooters. Congress should also take action, Horwitz writes, "to regulate high capacity magazines and accessories [such as bump stocks] that are designed to increase lethality." Such bans will save lives.

Disarm domestic abusers. Survivors of domestic violence need states and Congress to prohibit gun possession for those under temporary restraining orders. Congress should expand the definition of "intimate partner" to include dating partners. Simply put: those previously convicted of abuse or misdemeanor stalking should not have firearms.

Fund gun violence prevention research. As we saw in chapter 9, Congress's refusal to invest in research into gun violence has consequences. The Centers for Disease Control and Prevention need to research this public health crisis, and they need the funding to do it. Congress should also fund intervention programs. "Hospital intervention, Group Violence Interruption and other programs are emerging as effective avenues to reduce violence in the very communities where carnage has become commonplace," writes Horwitz. "By investing in these programs, our leaders will be investing in the safety of communities disproportionately impacted by gun violence."

To be sure, there will be more attempts at good legislation that will arise from time to time in our state assemblies, such as treating bump stocks like machine guns; repealing gun industry immunity; developing microstamping and safe-gun technology, and requiring buyers to be at least twenty-one years old before buying a gun, to name only a few. Such legislation deserves our support, and I hope you will agree to lift up your voice.

Next are some other changes for which you can advocate to your elected officials.

Demand the demilitarization of law enforcement and train cops in de-escalation

In the spirit of love, churches and concerned citizens should demand that police scale down their uniforms and equipment when they enter neighborhoods so that they do not look as if they are going to war. It is disadvantageous in the long run for the building of community for police forces to ride in military-grade armed personnel carriers, which police departments can acquire from the Pentagon free of charge. Surplus military armaments and weapons systems have no place in the hands of law enforcement. They are not soldiers; they are public servants. Police should not look like soldiers on city streets. Viable, safe communities cannot be built with threats of overwhelming force and military-grade weapons. Community is established through respectful dialogue, intentional relationship building, and interpersonal engagement. And we must insist that our police forces not only demilitarize their appearance but also de-escalate their tactics.

We should insist that our police and first responders carry nonlethal weapons (like stun guns) and that they have extensive training in de-escalating volatile situations. Every week we read of another police shooting that did not need to happen, and we hear the same tired statements that "the shooter feared for his life." According to the Police Executive Research Forum, new police cadets usually receive fifty-eight hours of firearms training, forty-nine hours in defensive skills, ten in communication skills, and only eight in de-escalation tactics.[4]

British cops, for example, are good at de-escalating tense situations because they are trained to do just that. Our police can learn a lot from their British bobby counterparts. American police who are in nail-biting situations are trained to draw their guns and to be decisive. They are told that to "back down" in confrontational situations is perceived as showing a lack of resolve and could be seen as a sign of weakness. We must ask, however, if "being so decisive" makes and keeps the peace.

Being decisive is a synonym for "being tough." And "being tough" is not only a police problem; it is an American predicament that leads to violence in hundreds of different guises. When police and gun owners feel they must always project a tough image, our homes, our streets, and our cities are endangered. More than anything else, our cops and all gun owners need to learn that the greatest power to change minds and hearts comes in the form of gentleness, empathy, and love.

Petition legislators for bail reform

The 2018 General Assembly of the Presbyterian Church (USA) meeting in St. Louis, Missouri, projected love in the most practical manner. The commissioners opted to focus on bail reform, a decades-old movement that has heated up in the host city in recent years after the shooting of Michael Brown in nearby Ferguson. The assembly collected $57,000 at its opening worship, and two days later hundreds of commissioners marched to the St. Louis City Justice Center to donate the offering to bail out people accused of minor, nonviolent offenses who could not pay their own bail. The Bail Project and ArchCity Defenders say that nearly two-thirds of people in St. Louis jails are awaiting trial, have not been convicted of any crime, and face only low-level, nonviolent charges. Those Presbyterians reasoned that the most loving thing they could do was help people return to their families and get back to work instead of languishing behind bars awaiting some distant trial.[5]

Citizens in our cities and towns might also try love. You can petition city councils to stop jailing people for minor offenses. Certainly there are many churches that would be willing to provide alternatives to incarceration. What if your church started a bail reform movement to benefit those arrested for nonviolent crime? Simple love and justice require empathy and compassionate hearts to fix broken systems. But by using our energy and creative imagination, we can discover new ways to demonstrate the gospel truth that each of us is a somebody whose very humanity must be respected.

Work to abolish for-profit prisons

One of the most important actions we can take is to join the movement to abolish for-profit private prisons. The goal of private prisons—to earn a profit for their shareholders—stands in fundamental conflict with what should be a central goal of the prison system: to rehabilitate those who offend and return them to society as productive citizens. This is a glaring and significant flaw, and for-profit private prisons should be abolished. The ultimate goal of the criminal justice system, according to the policies of faith groups in America, should be restorative justice, which concentrates on rehabilitation and reconciliation with victims and the community. The Presbyterian Church (USA) and other faith groups in America are united in calling for "changing a prison system that is based on the concept of punishment to one that encourages the restoration of the offender to the community and the development of alternatives to incarceration." The PCUSA statement on prisons expresses concern about the violent nature of prisons as institutions and expresses "the need to develop a nonpunitive philosophy that stresses the use of the least restrictive alternatives to imprisonment, including community-based corrections."[6]

Ban the box

"Have you been convicted by a court?" That question, which shows up on applications for jobs, housing, insurance, and loans, requires a check mark. You must answer either yes or no. Jobs are exactly what those who have been imprisoned need to find, and urban America already endures a profound lack of them. But for so many young African Americans labeled as felons because of time spent in prison for minor offenses, it is very difficult to find prospective employers willing to hire them. We have seen earlier the economic impact this question imposes on the poor. Both morally and economically, our nation cannot afford policies that force people who have already paid their debt to society to live the rest of their lives bearing the stigma of being known as a "felon." With that label, one can't find a good job or even receive food stamps.

All people of goodwill, but particularly those in faith communities, need to throw their moral weight behind the Ban the

Box campaign. Nationwide, more than thirty states and 150 cities and counties have adopted what is known as "ban the box" so that employers would consider a job candidate's qualifications first—"without the stigma of a conviction or arrest record." Efforts to "ban the box" provide applicants "a fair chance at employment by removing the conviction history question from job applications and delaying background checks until later in the hiring process." While interest in these policies has grown in recent years, we all know that progress in such efforts often moves with glacial speed.[7]

Talk to your church leaders about putting up a "gun-free zone" sign

I am a member of the Presbyterian Peace Fellowship. We worked long and hard to promote a program called No Guns in God's House, and our denomination's General Assembly endorsed it in 2014. Our national leaders asked congregations to post signs and decals that would bear witness to nonviolence and declare our sanctuaries free from violence and fear. Our *Gun Violence Prevention Congregational Toolkit* declares:

> Our denomination's efforts to affect change have been largely focused outside the church walls on advocacy and legislative change. Sadly, in 2013, we have seen how unwilling our legislators are to carry out the will of the American public regarding background checks and other laws that would restrict the ownership of assault weapons and ammunition. We believe that we need to provide a stronger witness by living out our commitment to nonviolence within our buildings and equipping members with resources to effect change in their local communities. Recent expanded provisions in concealed carry laws in many states now allow guns to be carried into places never before considered

appropriate, including houses of worship. It is important that our churches, at the grassroots level, stand firm against the deception that more guns in more places makes us somehow safer and more secure. . . . We hope that this signage will stimulate healthy and helpful conversation that will embolden congregations to witness for love and peace, and stand against fear.[8]

Love your neighbors rather than defend yourself against them

You may be feeling overwhelmed by now. The spiritual problem of guns in America is deeply entrenched and not easily defeated. But I'd encourage you to spend some time with this list of ideas for ways to show love and demand justice. See the resource list at the back of this book to connect with state- and national-level organizations that are working for common-sense gun laws. Consider other ways you feel called to act, and pray about which initiatives of love and justice you are energized to pursue. J. Herbert Nelson, the stated clerk of the Presbyterian Church (USA), reminds us, "It isn't enough to feel outrage, but do nothing. Or to feel fear, but do nothing. Or to feel utter, bone-crushing grief, but do nothing. We must institute policies that limit access to guns. Weapons of war have no place in our homes, communities, or law enforcement."[9]

Nelson depends on that call: "We as Church must confront the social sin of racism head-on," he says.

> We must get outside our church buildings, beyond our comfort zones, and say loudly and clearly, "This is my brother and I will not accept that his life is less valuable than mine. The violence has to stop." We must be willing to challenge the culture that tells African American boys that their lives are worth less than the lives of White boys. We live in a culture that attempts to justify itself

by claiming "self-defense" when we really mean fear and bigotry, or pride, or individualism. *But all of this is sin.* Our faith reminds us that God is all sovereign and that "God calls us to love our neighbors, not protect ourselves against our neighbors."[10]

FINDING HOPE

Working toward God's Peaceful Tomorrow

THOSE COMMITTED TO pursuing peace and justice in our communities live with a lot of tension. No matter the issue that keeps you up at night, it's likely that you sometimes feel that justice is doing anything but rolling down like waters. You might think that righteousness is not acting anything like the mighty stream that the prophet Amos foretold. Given the weight of the world's injustice, including the endless collateral damage of gun violence, you may feel a bit like the great civil rights activist Fannie Lou Hamer did when she said, "I'm sick and tired of being sick and tired."

Some of my family members and friends have considered my work against gun violence to be a strange calling; some have even called it "a crazy business." But I'm not in this work because it is pleasant to talk about. Nor is it because I succeed in persuading large numbers of citizens to join the movement. I do this work not because I receive lots of kudos. I am in it because God has put a burden on my heart to speak up. To borrow words from a beloved mentor, the late Paul Scherer, it's but the kind of burden that "sails are to a ship or wings are to a bird." I work to stop gun violence because it is the right, just, and loving thing to do. God wants me to do it, and that, in itself, brings me joy.

Grief makes up a large part of my work. How could it be otherwise? I've shed more than a few tears holding family members whose loved ones were mowed down by assault weapons. I grieve as I read of the pain and heartache similar violence brings to our communities every day. I'm distressed that our nation is led by a calloused, cowardly Congress that seems to perceive no tension between what is and what ought to be. But let no one suggest that joy rules out grieving. Joy manages to find me. In *The Hungering Dark*, writer Frederick Buechner sums it up this way: "Joy is a mystery because it can happen anywhere, anytime, even under the most unpromising circumstances, even in the midst of suffering, with tears in its eyes."[1]

So where can we find joy in this work? How can we hold on to hope when despair about gun violence nips always at our heels? I want to share some of the stories and truths that imbue me with hope and joy these days. In the face of the massive collateral damage that gun violence has visited upon millions, we need stories of transformation. We need confidence that the tomorrow God has planned for us is one of peace, not violence. We need hope.

Faith in Christ that offers hope

It took me a long time to realize that the church culture in which I was raised had bought into an artificial gospel. This gospel proclaimed that when one trusts in Jesus, peace like a river floods one's soul and all anxieties will cease. I used to beat myself up over that, because I never felt completely unruffled or calm. To the contrary, my experiences of God came as I listened to the One whom I call "the Great Disturber." My faith in God has never permitted me the luxury of being fully at peace—not when there were riots all across America; not when Black people were denied entrance to restaurants and toilets. How can one be calm and peaceful when there is a Vietnam or a Yemen or an American apartheid? How can one unequivocally claim "the peace of God that passes all understanding" when forty thousand Americans are killed every year by firearms? Does God want us unperturbed in such times? I don't think so. Perhaps that explains the comment of a psychiatrist who said, "Anyone who isn't tense these days probably isn't well." Although violence of any kind makes me uneasy, God wants me to do what little I can to stop the killing.

It took me some time to realize that my greatest tensions come because I trust God and try to live as Jesus lived. Simply *believing in Jesus* doesn't quite cut it. God wants me to *be* like Jesus. God wants me to *think and act* like Jesus and to *love* like Jesus. I try to make Paul's admonition to have the mind of Christ my North Star (Philippians 2:5).

In this fallen world, anyone who makes a conscious decision to follow Jesus of Nazareth, who was crucified, died, and was buried, lives with a tenuous hope that Jesus' way will prevail in this power-mad world. When we say "Jesus is Lord," we are declaring citizenship in a distinctly different commonwealth. By birth we are citizens of this earthly world; by faith we become adopted, naturalized citizens of the kingdom of God. Thus we are simultaneously claimed by the particular mores and morals of *both* cultures. We live with two sets of values, morals, and lifestyles that vie for our allegiance.

As a citizen of both commonwealths—the kingdom of God and a kingdom on this earth—I know a tension that claims my energy for the wrong reasons and keeps me in sync with the evil structures and systems of my earthly society. But thankfully, I also know a godly tension which, when acted upon, leads me to an authentic life and a closer walk with God. Therefore, my question is always, Will I trust and obey my Redeemer or my culture?

If you have tension in your life between what *is* and what *ought to be*, consider yourself blessed and happy! It is a sure sign that you belong to God. It is an indication that God's Spirit is working on you and working through you; it is God challenging you to put your muscles, your imagination, and your brains behind your prayers that God's kingdom would come on earth, even as it is in heaven. The most miraculous thing of all is that you and I can play a part in building God's kingdom.

The Greek word *makarios* can be translated "blessed," but I prefer the Greek vernacular: "happy." And what a collection of paradoxes God brings to our consciousness as we consider what biblical happiness means. These ironies are contradictory, almost unbelievable; they even sound absurd. But they are true. Each conundrum in the Beatitudes that Jesus shares in the Sermon on the Mount, recorded in Matthew 5, concludes with a promise of God's victory: a victory for truth, a victory for love and justice, a victory for the kingdom of God *on this earth*. The poor in spirit *will* receive the kingdom of heaven; those who mourn *will* be comforted; the meek *will* inherit the earth; those who hunger for righteousness *will* be filled; the merciful *will* receive mercy; the pure in heart *will* see God; the peacemakers *will* be called children of God (see Matthew 5:3-11). These are reliable promises from God proclaimed to all who are tense for the right reasons. To believe in God is to be a confirmed optimist, to be certain that what ought to be done *can and will* be done. Knowing that truth in the depths of my heart makes me joyful, even though gun violence can be so overwhelming.

Lives and testimonies that offer hope

Another reason I am a captive of hope is because I have seen with my own eyes the powerful, gracious way that victims of gun violence have salvaged the wreckage of their lives after a tragedy and lived to help others. The people I admire most are those who have suffered grievously and, through the grace and power of God, have made their suffering redemptive. They have made a conscious choice to turn their pain into healing the pain of others.

I think especially of the myriad friends and family members whose loved ones have been gunned down unnecessarily. Such folks usually have three choices as they move forward in life with a heartache that will never go away.

1. Victims of gun violence can do all in their power to persuade the courts to punish the perpetrators of the crime with the last full measure of retributive justice for their loss. They can live for the day when they watch their loved one's killer be led off in handcuffs to prison or the death chamber. Many choose this option, and we can listen to their invective on television. But one thing I do know: Without a change of heart, their pain and loathing will never diminish. It will haunt and control their psyches for the rest of their lives. They will never get over it; they will never be able to turn it loose.

2. Survivors of gun violence can choose forgiveness and grace. This radical response was demonstrated by an Old Order Amish community after a terrible mass shooting in 2006. In a one-room schoolhouse in Nickel Mines, Pennsylvania, gunman Charles Carl Roberts IV took hostage ten girls, ages six to

thirteen, and shot eight of them, killing five, before committing suicide. On the same day that the shooting occurred, members of the Amish community visited the shooter's family, offering grace and forgiveness and comfort even as they grieved the loss of their children. Here's how the authors of *Amish Grace* report that an Amish minister told part of the story:

> Well, there were three of us standing at the firehouse on Monday evening. We just thought we should go and say something to Amy, Roberts' widow. So first we went to her house, and no one was there. Then we walked over to her grandfather's house and no one was there. So we walked over to her father's house and she, her children, and parents were there alone. So we just talked with them for about ten minutes to express our sorrow and told them that we didn't hold anything against them.[2]

Over the next few days, more stories trickled out: about Amish people stopping by the house of Roberts's widow, bringing condolences and meals and flowers, and about the community starting a fund at a local bank to help the Roberts family. More than half the people who showed up for the funeral of the killer were Amish, including some of the parents whose daughters had been killed by Roberts.

Every time I read about this event, it takes my breath away. Imagine the America we would have should there be just a few more communities fortified with such love and the forgiveness of God. I will always marvel at the spiritual power of the Amish and their ability to forgive. They possess in abundance a spiritual authority I cannot claim. But knowing that such power is available to us all gives me hope for tomorrow.

3. Victims of gun violence can become politically and socially active. Many survivors I have admired through the years have simultaneously expressed both their rage at the proliferation

of guns and their commitment to somehow make their pain redemptive. I've been there with them on holy ground and watched as they throw their arms around new victims, whispering, "I know what you are going through. I've been there." One might think such folk would devote their time to trying to ban all guns. But they are very pragmatic, thoughtful people. They know that will never happen in America. Instead, they join organizations that fight gun violence. Some go into the ministry; others visit schools that have experienced violence and tell their stories to the youth. Some work with the police in community outreach; others act as go-betweens between gangs. Some establish relationships with the person who killed their own child and visit the person in prison; the strongest and the most loving among the survivors adopt the offender and bring him or her into their tight family circles.

You will find these victims at rallies and demonstrations wearing a picture of their loved one on a T-shirt or displayed on a big button. They lobby legislators and write letters to the editor. But the guiding principle of their lives, which I have heard them express hundreds of times, is "I will do whatever I can to keep others from experiencing the pain I have had to endure." That gives me hope for tomorrow. What does that do for you?

Organizations that offer hope

I have hope in God's future because of the many organizations and coalitions that have sprouted up of late and are working against gun violence (see the resource list on pages 191–99 for some of these). One of the most creative organizations was started by a gentle Mennonite man who was deeply troubled by all the gun deaths in his state of Colorado and throughout the United States. Michael Martin is a committed Mennonite pacifist who, six years ago, attended a Bible class. The class was studying the passage from Isaiah in which the prophet speaks of "the days to come" when people "shall beat their swords into plowshares, and their spears into pruning hooks; nation shall not lift up sword against nation, neither shall they learn war any more" (Isaiah 2:2, 4).

That ancient verse became a watchword for Martin. It soon was his calling: Martin knew God wanted him to become a blacksmith. He visited a neighbor who worked as a blacksmith and persuaded him to teach him his art. There were very few swords bringing death to Coloradans, but his state was full of guns that were taking the lives of his neighbors every day. He wanted to put them in the fire and turn them into garden tools that brought life instead of death.

Martin founded a nonprofit called RAWtools (RAW is *war* spelled backward). For six years he has expressed his faith in the nonviolent Jesus by turning this violent world around with the garden tools he has made from the barrels of guns. His business card describes his work as disarming hearts and forging peace. He, along with his friend, author Shane Claiborne, wrote a book called *Beating Guns: Hope for People Who Are Weary of Violence.* Martin particularly loves to beat the AK-47s and AR-15 assault weapons he gets into rakes and hand trowels. Go to his website, RAWtools.org, to find out more. Consider attending one of his sessions as he travels with his forge throughout the country "beating guns" and telling people of his nonviolent Christ.

The grassroots national movement that offers hope

"The only thing we can do is pray." I get so frustrated when I hear these words. I hear it often from people who have just learned that each day one hundred people die from guns, ten of whom are kids. When people sigh, "The only thing we can do is pray," it is often code for "There is nothing else we can do."

What a rejection of God's love! What a repudiation of God's will for our country. What a dismissal of discipleship and what a denial of the power of Christ in our lives!

Prayer that is unaccompanied by honest work to stop the violence and the killing is a cop-out. I am inviting you to do more than pray. I am inviting you to join a movement and get on board with a spiritual, moral, and ethical awakening.

Some of you may say, "This guy is delusional! Doesn't he read the papers? Doesn't he know the power of the NRA and the stranglehold gun extremists have on America?" But hold on a moment. Consider when movements begin. Movements begin not after resounding victories or in times or places of justice or peace. To the contrary: movements start with human pain, humiliation, and defeat as people cry out to God, "Why?" Does God actually want us to live this way? Movements start when things seem as if they can't get any worse.

Remember that bloody march for civil rights from Selma across the Edmund Pettus Bridge—the one that ended in utter defeat? Chaos reigned as white police officers on horseback beat Black marchers with billy clubs and turned dogs and water cannons on the defenseless. But that horrific event served as a spiritual awakening for white America that each human being has certain inalienable rights and that the rights of Black citizens were being systematically violated.

Recall as well the social movement that brought Big Tobacco to its knees. Tobacco was money in the bank for the rich, but it was systematically killing millions every year and condemning the masses to poor health and early graves. Big Tobacco is not dead. Yet today, with no-nonsense controls and regulations, tobacco companies cannot sell their poison indiscriminately, particularly to kids. This happened because regular citizens began to demand it.

Another movement took form as mothers who had buried children killed by drunk drivers organized. MADD, or Mothers Against Drunk Driving, convinced the nation that it was absurd to allow drunk drivers to command steering wheels without significant penalties and assurances. These moms demanded a sense of responsibility and changes in personal behavior, and they got it.

Today more and more people and coalitions are standing up to the NRA and gun extremists and speaking out against America's gun pandemic. There is more action and energy in this movement now than I have seen in my forty-five years of activism. New national organizations that are fighting gun violence have sprung up like daffodils in spring. One mass shooting after another after another is finally prompting thousands to act. Consider how dozens of faith communities have finally discovered that gun violence is, in fact, a spiritual and moral concern. Consider the ways that timid clergypersons, the NRA, and a cowardly Congress have been shamed by a society sick to death over their pious promises to hold the survivors of gun attacks "in our thoughts and prayers." The country is learning an essential lesson: thoughts and prayers are not enough!

The twentieth-century rabbi Abraham Joshua Heschel denounced irrelevant piety throughout his life and spent his days challenging the faith community to regard prayer as a force within the world rather than a spiritual exercise removed from it. He wrote, "Prayer is meaningless unless it is subversive, unless it seeks to overthrow and to ruin the pyramids of callousness, hatred, opportunism, falsehood."[3] The Jewish Theological Seminary, where Heschel taught, recently invited John Lewis, U.S. representative of Georgia's fifth congressional district, to deliver the commencement address. Not only Rabbi Heschel but the prophet Micah would have been pleased to hear Lewis challenge the graduates to "find a way to get in trouble . . . good trouble, necessary trouble."[4]

Consider the power that resides in 92 percent of the American people, including numerous NRA members, who stand ready for some "necessary trouble" and are demanding that we have background checks for all guns sold! That's the beginning of a movement. And what about individual states that are not waiting for Congress and are making their own laws that regulate guns? Ponder the fact that gun violence is no longer the third rail of politics and that the Democratic Party flipped the majority of seats in the 2018 elections, where many of these newly elected representatives ran on gun issues. Consider that we've never before had a real, honest-to-goodness grassroots movement against gun violence in this country. We've had a few successes every now and then, such as a few one-gun-a-month laws and several states raising the age for gun ownership to twenty-one. Yet we have never had a sustained, broad-based movement.

We have one now.

Before the telephone, the quickest communication was the telegraph. In those days, as the story goes, a young man left home to seek fame and fortune in Chicago. But times were harder than he expected. With dwindling cash in his wallet, the young man telegraphed his father: "Alone in Chicago without money and without friends. Advise." His father telegraphed back: "Find friends immediately."

We who work for safer communities have taken that advice and have found a lot of friends—and influential ones too! High on our list is law enforcement, which is solidly behind our efforts to close the gun show loophole and keep assault weapons out of dangerous hands. The NRA elite and gundamentalists like to parade a sheriff or police officer or two in front of their

188 / COLLATERAL DAMAGE

well-guarded microphones, but law enforcement across the board supports the actions and policies of the faith communities. After all, they are our first responders. There are coalitions of mayors and police chiefs all across the country who are solidly behind us. Doctors and nurses and others in the medical community, particularly those who work in emergency departments and try to patch up bodies riddled with bullets, are very good friends to the movement. Those with the unenviable task of telling families that their dear ones did not make it are becoming increasingly active in this work.

There are growing lists of pastors and priests, rabbis and imams, and leaders of every religion who are on call. Psychologists, social workers, and personal counselors know the temptations of resorting to violence and its dead-end street. They can provide much better solutions to human conflict. Teachers, as well as a growing number of victims, want to help get the word out, and they have compelling testimonies.

Working for God's tomorrow

The movement to end gun violence is gaining steam, and the church must be at the heart of it. The movement is all about specific actions, like those listed above, that bring love, hope, healing, and shalom to those who have suffered death, injury, and shattering loss. Each action is, in essence, the result of the empathy of God's people prompted by God's Spirit. I am convinced that this grassroots movement is a kairos moment—the evidence of God's work in the world today. God's peaceful society is on the way.

The movement is coming your way, and you can join in or watch it pass you by. Jesus, too, was always moving on, traveling to more cities and more towns. "I must preach the good news of the kingdom of God to the other cities also," he said; "for I was sent for this purpose" (Luke 4:43). Are you ready to climb on board this spiritual movement to stop the violence? Are you ready to do whatever it takes to stop the killing? Are you ready to help build the kingdom of God *on earth*?

Wouldn't it be great if the church of Jesus Christ stepped out front to stop the killing? After all, God created the church to be salt, yeast, and light to this world, not to march in lock-step behind the corporate gun lobby. God calls the church to obey Jesus' words even when, or *particularly* when, they conflict with the dictates of this earthly commonwealth. God created the church to lead—out front—and to bear witness to the love and justice our Lord described in Matthew 5 and 25. The almighty God did not commission us to serve as a mirror for a self-seeking, self-serving society. God created us to be a light in the darkness, which the darkness cannot extinguish (John 1:5).

I must admit that I get discouraged about the violence from time to time. When I despair and need some renewed energy, I frequently turn to a paragraph in the Declaration of Faith that was adopted by the Presbyterian Church, US, in the 1970s:

> The people of God have often misused God's promises
> as excuses for doing nothing about present evils.
> But in Christ the new world has already broken in
>   and the old can no longer be tolerated.
> We know our efforts cannot bring in God's kingdom.
> But hope plunges us into the struggle
>   for victories over evil that are possible now
>   in the world, the church, and our individual lives.
> Hope gives us courage and energy
>   to contend against all opposition,
>   however invincible it may seem,
>   for the new world and the new humanity
>   that are surely coming.

Jesus is Lord!
He has been Lord from the beginning.
He will be Lord at the end.
Even now he is Lord.[5]

The concrete actions of God's committed people can and always will, in the providence of God, bear good fruit. What we do in God's name, what we do for the sake of truth, what we do for love, what we do to seek the welfare of our cities and all their peoples: all these things matter to God.

Despite his youth, a junior high school student in a confirmation class understood that hope. The young people were discussing Jesus' petition in the Lord's Prayer: "Your kingdom come, your will be done, on earth as it is in heaven." The minister asked the class, "What is the kingdom of God?" The young man volunteered: "I think it's God's tomorrow, which is kind of here today already."

When all is said and done, we are working for God's peaceful tomorrow: that breathtaking day when pain, suffering, and death are no more and when violence is erased. May God's tomorrow, which is "kind of here today already," truly come.

Resource List

This list of national and regional groups was created by the Presbyterian Peace Fellowship (PPF) Gun Violence Prevention Ministry. See www.presbypeacefellowship.org/gun-violence.

National groups

Coalition to Stop Gun Violence

www.csgv.org; 202-408-0061

Founded in 1974 and based in Washington, D.C., this coalition of forty-seven national organizations is one of the largest groups working on education and policy to prevent gun violence. The Presbyterian Church (USA) is a member; *Collateral Damage* author Rev. James Atwood is on the national board of directors. Associated with the CSVG: The Educational Fund to Stop Gun Violence.

Everytown for Gun Safety

www.everytown.org; 646-324-8250

Created from a merger in 2013 of Moms Demand Action for Gun Sense in America and Mayors Against Illegal Guns, Everytown has contacts in every state in the United States, with an "every state" strategy for saving lives. Everytown promotes National Gun Violence Awareness Day in June, asking Americans to wear orange and to create local events to raise awareness. Its networks include **Moms Demand Action**, **Students Demand Action**, **Everytown Survivor Network**, and **Mayors Against Illegal Guns**.

March for Our Lives

www.marchforourlives.com

Launched by students after the February 2018 school shooting in Parkland, Florida, March for Our Lives inspired an estimated two million people to participate in events nationwide on March 24, 2018, and in a massive voter registration campaign among teens and young adults. See information on how teens can start a Local Activism Club, the Vote for Our Lives project, and school walkouts to protest inaction by adults to reform gun regulation. "America's mass shooting generation is mobilizing."

Brady Campaign to Prevent Gun Violence

www.bradyunited.org; 202-370-8100

Founded by Jim and Sarah Brady and sponsor of the Million Mom March in 2000, the Brady Campaign has launched a goal to cut American gun deaths in half by 2025 through a combination of public policy, safety, and public awareness changes. Based in Washington D.C., they also sponsor the Legal Action Project to use the court system to support sensible gun policy. With ninety-four chapters across the United States, they maintain an online map that shows local affiliates across the nation. Their website offers worship resources under "God not Guns."

States United to Prevent Gun Violence

www.ceasefireusa.org or www.supgv.org

Established in 2010 to create a fifty-state solution to gun violence and as a clearinghouse on state gun laws and advocacy efforts. So far they have networks in thirty-two states and can help you get started in your state. Programs include safe gun storage to prevent child gun deaths and support for steps to prevent domestic gun violence against women.

Giffords

www.giffords.org

Founded by Gabby Giffords and Mark Kelly in 2012 as Americans for Responsible Solutions, Giffords now sponsors education, advocacy, a political action committee, and the Giffords Law Center to Prevent Gun Violence. The law center has worked for more than twenty years to mobilize lawyers to help strengthen gun laws. Topics covered range from universal background checks to gun design safety and standards to regulations on reporting lost and stolen guns. The Giffords Law Center maintains an online resource and scorecard on the gun laws in each of the U.S. states. Select your state to find current regulations at www.smartgunlaws.org/search-gun-law-by-state.

Newtown Action Alliance

www.newtownactionalliance.org

Founded in Newtown, Connecticut, after the 2012 Sandy Hook school shooting, the Newtown Action Alliance exists to "provide comfort, education, scholarship and other support and resources to people and communities impacted by or living in the aftermath of gun violence in American society, and to help them lead the way toward positive cultural change." Actions include efforts to reduce the use of violence in entertainment and to ask politicians to refrain from accepting donations from the NRA.

Gun Violence Archive

www.gunviolencearchive.org

Provides free public access to accurate reporting on gun-related incidents in America, updated daily. Not an advocacy group, GVA gathers near real-time data from over two thousand media, law enforcement, government, and commercial sources daily. Results are published at www.facebook.com/gunviolencearchive.

Sandy Hook Promise

www.sandyhookpromise.org

Founded after the Sandy Hook school shooting, Sandy Hook Promise seeks to find middle ground in the search for solutions, with a focus on community-based mental health and crisis intervention programs, as well as on legislation to allow law enforcement to temporarily remove guns from individuals deemed a danger to themselves or others.

Faiths United to Prevent Gun Violence

www.faithsunited.org

Created by more than fifty national religious groups that have agreed to work together on projects to lessen the grip of the gun industry, including sponsoring the Gun Violence Prevention Sabbath. Their website's "Other Resources" section includes the excellent *Gun Violence*

194 / COLLATERAL DAMAGE

Guide for Faith Leaders. PPF and the Presbyterian Church (USA) are members of Faiths United.

Violence Policy Center

www.vpc.org

Investigates and analyzes accurate statistics on gun violence, information on the gun industry, and research-based steps to prevent gun violence. Topics range from murder-suicide to self-defense gun use.

Regional groups

Gun violence prevention contacts in all fifty states are listed here. In addition, national groups with chapters in most states include March for Our Lives (www.marchforourlives.com/chapters), Moms Demand Action (www.momsdemandaction.org), and States United to Prevent Gun Violence (www.ceasefireusa.org/affiliates).

Alabama

Moms Demand Action AL, www.facebook.com/
    MomsDemandActionAL

Alaska

We Are Anchorage, https://www.facebook.com/WeAreAnchorage
Moral Movement, www.moralmovementAK.org

Arizona

Arizonans for Gun Safety, www.azfgs.com
Gun Violence Prevention Arizona, www.gvparizona.org

Arkansas

Brady Campaign of Arkansas, centralarkansas@bradymail.org
Moms Demand Action AR, www.facebook.com/
    MomsDemandAction/AR

California

Women Against Gun Violence, www.wagv.org
Americans Against Gun Violence, www.aagunv.org
University of California at Davis Violence Prevention Research
    Program, www.ucdmc.ucdavis.edu/vprp

Colorado

Colorado Ceasefire, www.coloradoceasefire.org

Hunters Against Gun Violence,
www.huntersagainstgunviolence.com

Faith Communities United to End Gun Violence,
www.cfcu-co.org

Connecticut

Connecticut Against Gun Violence, www.cagv.org

Delaware

Delaware Coalition Against Gun Violence, www.decagv.org

Florida

Florida Coalition to Prevent Gun Violence,
www.preventgunviolenceflorida.org

Georgia

Georgians for Gun Safety, www.gunsafetygeorgia.org

Outcry Georgia, Interfaith Group, www.outcrygeorgia.org

Hawaii

Hawaii Coalition to Prevent Gun Violence (on Facebook)

Idaho

Moms Demand Action ID, www.facebook.com/
MomsDemandActionID

Illinois

Illinois Council Against Handgun Violence, www.ichv.org

Illinois Gun Violence Prevention Coalition, www.ilgvp.com

Indiana

Hoosiers Concerned About Gun Violence, www.hcgv.org

Iowa

Iowans for Gun Safety, www.facebook.com/IA4GS

Kansas

Grandparents Against Gun Violence, www.moksgagv.org

Aim4Peace Violence Prevention Program, www.kcmo.gov/health/aim4peace

Kentucky

Sowers of Justice Network, Louisville, www.sowersofjusticenetwork.org/nonviolence

Louisiana

LA Coalition against Domestic Violence, www.lcadv.org

Louisiana Violence Reduction Coalition, www.laviolencereduction.org

Maine

Maine Gun Safety Coalition, www.mainegunsafety.org

Maryland

Marylanders to Prevent Gun Violence, www.mdpgv.org

Massachusetts

Massachusetts Coalition to Prevent Gun Violence, www.mapreventgunviolence.org

Stop Handgun Violence, www.stophandgunviolence.org

Michigan

Coalition for Common Ground, www.facebook.com/CCGKZOO

Michigan Coalition to Prevent Gun Violence, www.facebook.com/MichiganCoalitiontoPreventGunViolence

Minnesota

Protect Minnesota, www.protectmn.org

Mississippi

Moms Demand Action MS, www.facebook.com/momsdemandactionMS

Missouri

Grandparents Against Gun Violence, www.moksgagv.org

Saint Louis Story Stitchers, www.storystitchers.org/portfolio/gun-violence-prevention

Women's Voices Raised for Social Justice, www.womensvoicesraised.org/gun-solutions

Montana

Helena Youth Against Gun Violence, www.twitter.com/hyagv
Big Sky Rising, www.facebook.com/pg/BigSkyRising
Jeanette Rankin Peace Center, Missoula, www.jrpc.org

Nebraska

Nebraskans Against Gun Violence, www.nagv.org

Nevada

Moms Demand Action NV, www.facebook.com/
    MomsDemandActionNV

New Hampshire

New Hampshire Firearm Safety Coalition, www.theconnectprogram
    .org/resources/nh-firearm-safety-coalition
Granite State Progress, www.facebook.com/granite.progress

New Jersey

Ceasefire NJ, www.peacecoalition.org/campaigns/ceasefire.html
Rutgers Center on Gun Violence Research, https://
    gunviolenceresearchcenter.rutgers.edu
Women for Progress, www.womenforprogress.org/gun-violence
    -prevention

New Mexico

New Mexicans to Prevent Gun Violence,
    www.newmexicanstopreventgunviolence.org

New York

New Yorkers Against Gun Violence, www.nyagv.org
Mayor's Office to Prevent Gun Violence (NYC), www.nyc.gov/
    peacenyc

North Carolina

North Carolinians Against Gun Violence, www.ncgv.org
League of Women Voters of North Carolina, www.lwvnc.org/act/
    league-action-items/gun-violence-prevention

North Dakota
Moms Demand Action ND, www.facebook.com/
momsdemandactionND

Ohio
Ohio Coalition Against Gun Violence, www.ohioceasefire.org
God Before Guns, www.godbeforeguns.org
Patriots for Change, www.patriotsforchangechagrinvalley.org

Oklahoma
OKGunSense (on Facebook)
Moms Demand Action OK, www.facebook.com/
MomsDemandActionOK

Oregon
Ceasefire Oregon, www.ceasefireoregon.org
Oregon Youth for Gun Reform, www.busproject.org/campaign/oyfgr

Pennsylvania
CeaseFire PA, www.ceasefirepa.org
Heeding God's Call (Philadelphia, Pittsburgh, Harrisburg),
www.heedinggodscall.org
Delaware County United for Sensible Gun Policy,
www.delcounited.net
Bucks Against Gun Violence, www.facebook.com/BucksAGV

Rhode Island
Rhode Island Coalition Against Gun Violence, www.ricagv.org

South Carolina
Arm-in-Arm: South Carolinians for Responsible Gun Ownership,
www.arminarmsc.org

South Dakota
Moms Demand Action SD, www.facebook.com/
MomsDemandActionSD

Tennessee
Safe Tennessee Project, www.safetennesseeproject.org

Texas

Texas Gun Sense, www.txgunsense.org

Moms Demand Action TX, www.facebook.com/
    momsdemandactionTX

Utah

Gun Violence Prevention Center of Utah, www.gvpc.org

Gun Sense Utah, www.facebook.com/gunsense.action

Vermont

Gun Sense Vermont, http://www.gunsensevt.org

Virginia

Virginia Center for Public Safety, www.vacps.org

Northern Virginia Coalition Against Gun Violence, https://www
    .facebook.com/NorthernVirginiaBrady

Washington

Grandmothers Against Gun Violence, www.
    grandmothersagainstgunviolence.org

Alliance for Gun Responsibility Foundation, www.foundation
    .gunresponsibility.org

Washington CeaseFire, www.washingtonceasefire.org

West Virginia

Moms Demand Action WV, www.facebook.com/
    MomsDemandActionWV

Wisconsin

Wisconsin Anti-Violence Effort, www.waveedfund.org

Wyoming

Moms Demand Action WY, www.facebook.com/
    momsdemandactionwy

Acknowledgments

OFTEN SAY THAT my wife, Roxana, is disgustingly healthy. But I am also intensely proud of her discipline, at eighty-two years of age, of getting up every morning while it is still dark and walking four to five miles. I, on the other hand, love to sleep late. If there is such a thing as reincarnation, I will return as a three-toed sloth.

When I wake up every morning, at least for the last six years in a retirement community, my first words are an important question: "Are you here, dear?" Roxana is usually back from her walk by that time and is working at the computer. When I hear her reply, "Yes, I am," it is like music and magic to my ears.

I have been incredibly blessed to have had her here by my side for sixty years. For the last forty-five years I have spent trying to prevent gun violence, my wife has been "right here." She has read and made suggestions for corrections to my papers, listened to my sermons and speeches, joined me at the same rallies and demonstrations, laughed at the same old jokes, and helped me in countless ways to hang in there fighting gun violence, which I believe is America's greatest spiritual, moral, and ethical problem. Thank you, dear heart, for always being *here* for me. It is not hyperbole when I say that I could not have done it without you.

My son, Harry David, and daughter, Mebane, and grandsons and granddaughters have also been a constant source of love and support—and I include in those categories my so-called in-laws, who are dear to my heart. I can't tell you the joy I experience when I hear one of them speak up or write about supporting sound, reasonable laws that would stop the killing. Thank you!

In writing this book, I have once again been the beneficiary of the insights, wisdom, and counsel not only of family, but of good friends and colleagues who champion this cause. I think particularly of my pastor, Stephanie Sorge, and the gutsy members of Trinity Presbyterian Church of Harrisonburg, Virginia, and the hundreds of faithful citizens who show up on the fourteenth day of every month—the date of the Sandy Hook Elementary School shooting, in which twenty first graders were murdered—at the headquarters of the NRA in Fairfax County, Virginia. We lift up our voices to protest the work of the corporate gun lobby that has blood on its hands. We lift up our signs to bear witness to Virginia and the entire country that we do not have to live this way.

One might think a retirement community would be rather docile, its members reluctant or unable to stand up and speak out against violence. Not the community at Sunnyside! I'm particularly grateful for my "Rationalist Friends" who meet once a month to discuss what's important. Thanks to Jim Kellett, Charlie Lotts, Tip Parker, Don Oxley, Charlie Shank, and Dick Francis. I'm also grateful to the "GOP" (Good Old Progressives), who are always eager to learn what is going on in the world and take action. We attend demonstrations, write dozens of letters, and make telephone calls to our representatives. Thank you for your perseverance, which is an inspiration. Many thanks to Bill Marlowe, a friend of many years, who continues to keep my computer running. I also want to extend special thanks to special friends with whom my wife and I share so much: Bill and Nancy Caperton, Andy and Frances Sale, John and Ann Speer, and Pat Bertoia.

I express gratitude to all my colleagues of the Presbyterian Peace Fellowship and particularly its Gun Violence Task Force. For years they have been a devoted and unwavering source of bright ideas and creativity in leading our denomination to take bold action steps to stop the killing. I'm unable to name them all, but I'm especially thankful for its chairperson, Rev. Margery Rossi, and for Rev. Jan Orr-Harter, both of whom have made significant contributions to this book.

I'm so humbled and thankful for faith leaders in many denominations and states who have read my books or others of a similar vein and started city or statewide organizations or discussion groups and Sunday school classes to learn about the issue and to take action. Thank you to those who "gently pushed" their pastors to preach on the topic. I'm compelled to mention Rev. John Mathison, who, in his nineties, "always shows up" and has been a staunch defender and benefactor of the movement. He has kept the issue alive every place he has lived.

I've been encouraged and motivated by the work of the Northern Virginia Coalition Against Gun Violence, led by Martina Leinz. She and the members are ubiquitous as they lend their voices and put their bodies on the line to support reasonable gun laws that would save lives. Worthy of exceptional praise in the Coalition's work are the three Unitarian Universalist congregations in Fairfax County *who for six years have shown up* on the fourteenth of every month at NRA headquarters. Special thanks to Rev. David

204 / COLLATERAL DAMAGE

Miller (UU Congregation of Fairfax) and Rev. Dr. Kate Walker (Mount Vernon Unitarian Church).

I'm especially grateful for the work of Robert Hatfield and Gerry Poje, who lead these monthly efforts along with Joanna Simon, Kris Gregory, Carol Luten, Ben Zuhl, Cecile Heatley, Kevin Bergen, and Karen Higa.

Shortly after I began work with the National Coalition to Stop Gun Violence in 1975, we went through a few years when we didn't know if we could survive. Today, under the leadership of Josh Horwitz and a very active board of directors and new staff, we are going strong and lead the larger national movement in creative, evidence-based approaches that save lives. I'm grateful especially to Josh and his talented staff and especially for the privilege of continuing to serve on their board.

When I have questions about what is happening in gun violence prevention, or what the Virginia legislature is considering, I call Lori Haas of the Coalition, or Andy Goddard, both of whom are parents of survivors of Virginia Tech. Thanks, Lori and Andy, for always being there for me, and for arming me with facts.

Special thanks to former co-moderator of the Presbyterian Church (USA) (2016–17), and now the coordinator for Racial and Cultural Justice for the PCUSA, Rev. Denise Anderson, and to Rev. Alonso Johnson, coordinator of the Self-Development of Peoples Program, who gave me valuable advice on issues of race and urban America that are manifest in several of my chapters.

Special thanks to my good friend, Rev. Dr. J. Herbert Nelson, the stated clerk of the PCUSA General Assembly, who graciously agreed to write the foreword. I am honored and humbled to count J. Herbert as my trusted friend and colleague. The PCUSA is blessed to have him at the helm of our denomination.

When the rubber hit the road and I needed editorial support, Luisa Miller came to my rescue. And even though she made me work harder than I had anticipated on my many endnotes, I am grateful for her guidance and her holding my feet to the fire. Thanks, Luisa.

Special kudos are reserved for the acquisitions editor, Valerie Weaver-Zercher, with whom it was such a privilege to work. She taught me so much about writing with her gracious and gentle manner. I read once of a famous writer, whose name escapes me, who apologized to his friend for sending a long letter. "I didn't have time to make it shorter," he said. Valerie taught me by example that writing is sometimes like praying. We are not heard for the numbers of words we put on paper. I take full responsibility for all the words in this book. But when you run into sentences and paragraphs that speak truth and ring with authentic, creative language expressed in just a few words, you can bet that Valerie's guiding hand has been at work. Thank you, Valerie, from the heart!

Nor did I expect to be so blessed when I was introduced to a copyeditor for Herald Press, Sara Versluis, a gentle but knowledgeable critic who has shepherded my book through its final phases. How grateful I am to have had the privilege of working with Sara for the final push in getting this book to the printer. And finally, I must also thank all those at Herald Press who have gone the extra mile to make *Collateral Damage* a reality.

Notes

Foreword

1   Advisory Committee on Social Witness Policy, *Gun Violence, Gospel Values: Mobilizing in Response to God's Call* (The Office of the General Assembly of the Presbyterian Church USA, 2011).

Chapter 1

1   Statistics in this paragraph are from Everytown for Gun Safety and the Centers for Disease Control and Prevention.

2   Christopher Ingraham, "There Are More Guns Than People in the United States, according to a New Study of Global Firearm Ownership," *Washington Post*, June 19, 2018, https://www.washingtonpost.com/news/wonk/wp/2018/06/19/there-are-more-guns-than-people-in-the-united-states-according-to-a-new-study-of-global-firearm-ownership.

3   On number of firearms manufactured in 2016: Bureau of Alcohol, Tobacco, Firearms and Explosives, "Annual Firearms Manufacturing and Export Report, Year 2016 Final" January 4, 2018, https://www.atf.gov/about/docs/undefined/afmer2016webreport508pdf/download; other data from Bureau of Alcohol, Tobacco, Firearms, and Explosives, "Firearms Commerce in the United States—Annual Statistical Update 2017," https://www.atf.gov/resource-center/docs/undefined/firearms-commerce-united-states-annual-statistical-update-2017/download.

4   Ed Pelkington, "Gun Deaths in US Rise to Highest Level in 20 Years, Data Shows," *The Guardian*, December 13, 2018.

5   *Webster's New World College Dictionary*, 5th ed. (2014), s.v. "collateral damage."

6   Arthur Kellerman, "Guns for Safety? Dream On, Scalia," *Washington Post*, June 29, 2008.

7   As cited by Charles Blow, "A Funeral in Ferguson," *New York Times*, August 24, 2014.

8   Associated Press, "Newtown Dad Dies in Apparent Suicide," *Daily News-Record* (Harrisonburg, VA), March 26, 2019.

9   Melissa Chan, "The Poison in Their Blood," Time, July 8, 2019, 40–43.

10   Lisa Hamp, "I Survived a Mass Shooting. My Life Has Never Been the Same," *Washington Post*, February 18, 2018.

11   Julia Burdick-Will, "Neighborhood Violence, Peer Effects and Academic Achievement in Chicago," *Sociology of Education* 91, no. 3 (June 12, 2018): 207.

12   Pelkington, "Gun Deaths in US."

Chapter 2

1   *Webster's New World College Dictionary*, 5th ed. (2014), s.v. "myth."

2   John F. Kennedy (commencement address, New Haven, CT, Yale University, June 11, 1962).

3   Robert Preidt, "How U.S. Gun Deaths Compare to Other Countries," CBS News, February 3, 2016.

4   Sandro Galea and David Vlakov, "Social Determinants and the Health of Drug Users: Socioeconomic Status, Homelessness, and Incarceration," *Public Health Reports* 117 (2002): S135; American Psychological Association, *Gun Violence: Prediction, Prevention, and Policy* (Washington, DC: APA, 2013), https://www.apa.org/pubs/info/reports/gun-violence-report.pdf.

5   Preidt, "How U.S. Gun Deaths."

6   Alex Yablon, "The 12 Reasons Why Americans Fail Federal Gun Background Checks," The Trace, updated February 28, 2019, https://www.thetrace.org/2015/07/gun-background-checks-nics-failure/.

7   Alex Yablon, "More Good Guys with Concealed Guns = More Violent Crime," The Trace, June 29, 2017, https://www.thetrace.org/2017/06/right-to-carry-crime-stats/.

8   Jon Levine, "An NRA Official Just Blamed a Charleston Victim for His Own Death," Mic, June 19, 2015, https://mic.com/articles/121003/nra-official-clementa-pinckney-charleston-church-shooting.

9   Christopher Ingraham, "For Many Mass Shooters, Armed Guards Aren't a Deterrent, They're Part of the Fantasy," *Washington Post*, March 1, 2018.

10   "More Guns, More Shootings: Better Medical Care Has Kept Gun Death Constant, but Total Number of People Shot Has Risen Dramatically in the United States," Violence Policy Center, January 8, 2012, http://vpc.org/studies/moreguns.pdf.

11   John Woodrow Cox et al., "More Than 219,000 Students Have Experienced Gun Violence since Columbine," *Washington Post*, October 29, 2018.

12   "Number of Murder Victims in the US in 2017, by Weapon," Statista: The Statistics Portal, https://www.statista.com/statistics/195325/murder-victims-in-the-us-by-weapon-used/.

13 Cited monthly in the *American Rifleman Magazine*, 10.

14 According to the Gun Violence Archive—"the most comprehensive and systematic effort to catalog every publicly available defensive gun use [DGU] report"—there were fewer than 1,600 DGUs in 2014. "Pro-gun advocates have been forced to argue that the reason researchers can barely find .064 percent of the 2.5 million DGUs a year claimed by Kleck and [Mark] Gertz is because virtually nobody reports their defensive gun use to the police."

"The only thing known is what the data shows: Namely, there is a reliable floor for defensive gun use estimates at around 1,600 a year. In addition, according to the most recent data on defensive gun use, we have reliable evidence showing that owning a firearm does *not* give individuals any significant advantage in a criminal confrontation, and they are no less likely to lose property or be injured by using a gun in self-defense." Evan Defilappis and Devin Hughes, "Gunfight or Flee: New Study Finds No Advantages to Using a Firearm in Self-Defense Situations," The Trace, January 19, 2016, emphasis added. The reader is further directed to numerous studies by David Hemenway of Harvard University.

15 Arthur Kellerman, "Guns for Safety? Dream On, Scalia," *Washington Post*, June 29, 2008.

16 Mike Spies and Emily Fuhrman, "Watch How Chicago Gets Flooded with Thousands of Crime Guns," The Trace, November 2, 2015.

17 "Indiana Gun Laws," Giffords Law Center to Prevent Gun Violence, accessed April 17, 2019, https://lawcenter.giffords.org/gun-laws/state-law/indiana/.

18 Tom Diaz, *Making a Killing: The Business of Guns in America* (New York: New Press, 1999), 126.

19 Ibid., 64.

Chapter 3

1 Adam Winkler, *Gunfight: The Battle over the Right to Bear Arms in America* (New York: W.W. Norton, 2011), 165.

2 Ibid., x.

3 Osha Gray Davidson, *Under Fire: The NRA and the Battle for Gun Control* (Iowa City: University of Iowa Press, 1998), 30.

4 Ibid., 36.

5 Ibid., 44.

6 Ibid., 36.

7 James E. Atwood, *Gundamentalism and Where It Is Taking America* (Eugene, OR: Wipf and Stock, 2017), 37.

8 It should not go unnoticed that as of this writing, the NRA is dealing with corruption inside their ranks and their CEO is busy explaining his six-figure spending on clothing and travel expenses. Tim Mak, "As Leaks Show Lavish NRA Spending, Former Staff Detail Poor Conditions at Nonprofit," NPR, May 15, 2019.

9   Tom Kertscher, "A Mostly on Target Claim: 97 Percent of Gun Owners Support Universal Background Checks," PolitiFact Wisconsin, March 2, 2018, www.politifact.com/wisconsin/statements/2018/mar/02/ tammy-baldwin/mostly-target-claim-97-percent-gun-owners-support-/.

10   James E. Atwood, *America and Its Guns: A Theological Exposé* (Eugene, OR: Cascade Books, 2012), 151.

11   Marilynne Robinson, "This Cruel Parody of Representation," *The Nation*, January 12, 2018, 1–2.

12   "The Excuse for Reckless Violence," *Washington Post*, August 10, 2018.

13   Ibid. After the county sheriff decided not to bring charges, Drejka was charged with manslaughter by the Florida state attorney.

14   Peter Hermann, "Anne Arundel Police Consider New Gear, Weapons, to Confront Active Shooters after Capital Gazette Shooting," *Capital Gazette*, July 20, 2018.

15   Leila Fadel, "U.S. Hate Groups Rose 30 Percent in Recent Years, Watchdog Group Reports," NPR's *All Things Considered*, February 20, 2019, https://www.npr.org/2019/02/20/696217158/u-s-hate-groups-rose-sharply -in-recent-years-watchdog-group-reports.

16   John Eligon, "Hate Crimes Increase for Third Consecutive Year, FBI Reports," *New York Times*, November 13, 2018.

17   Walter Brueggemann, *Genesis*, Interpretation: A Bible Commentary (Atlanta: John Knox Press, 1980), 32.

18   C. S. Lewis, *The Screwtape Letters* (New York: HarperCollins, 2009), 160. First published 1942. Emphasis in the original.

19   Peter W. Marty, "What Drives Hate," *Christian Century*, January 4, 2017.

20   "U.S. Gun Death Rate Jumps 17 Percent since 2008 Supreme Court *District of Columbia v. Heller* Decision Affirming Right to Own a Handgun for Self-Defense," Violence Policy Center, January 17, 2018. According to the Violence Policy Center, "state gun death rates are calculated by dividing the number of gun deaths by the total state population and multiplying the result by 100,000 to obtain the rate per 100,000, which is the standard and accepted method for comparing fatal levels of gun violence."

21   The Gun Violence Archive (www.GunViolenceArchive.org) is the premier source of gun violence statistics in America. It archives gun violence incidents from over twenty-five hundred law enforcement, media, government, and commercial sources.

22   R. M. C. Kagawa et al., "Firearms Involvement in Violent Victimization and Mental Health: An Observational Study," *Annals of Internal Medicine* 169, no. 8 (2018): 584–85.

23   "Trauma after Gun Violence," Vantage Point, accessed May 14, 2019, https://vantagepointrecovery.com/trauma-gun-violence/.

24   *Terrorist Watchlist Screening: Before the Senate Comm. on Homeland Security and Governmental Affairs*, 111th Cong. (2010) (testimony of

Eileen R. Larance, director of Homeland Security and Justice Issues, Government Accountability Office).

Chapter 4

1 Nolan Stout, "Page Man Charged with Shooting," *Daily News-Record* (Harrisonburg, VA), May 30, 2018.

2 Pete DeLea, "Police: City Man Shot at Car," *Daily News-Record* (Harrisonburg, VA), July 23, 2018.

3 Quoted in Joe Setyon, "Rudy Giuliani Defends Claim That Truth Isn't Truth," *Hit and Run* (blog), *Reason*, August 20, 2018, https://reason.com/blog/2018/08/20/rudy-giuliani-defends-claim-that-truth-i.

4 Quoted in George Will, "The Wisdom of Pat Moynihan," *Washington Post*, October 3, 2010.

5 Wayne LaPierre (speech, Conservative Political Action Conference, Washington, DC, February 27, 2009).

6 Joshua Horwitz and Casey Anderson, *Guns, Democracy, and the Insurrectionist Idea* (Ann Arbor: University of Michigan Press, 2009), 26–27.

7 *Frontline*, season 7, episode 6, "Trump's Takeover," directed by Michael Kirk, written by Michael Kirk and Mike Wiser, aired April 10, 2018, on PBS.

8 Ben Steelman, "New Hanover Task Force Plans to Deal with ACEs in Children's Lives," *Wilmington (NC) Star News*, July 26, 2018, www.starnewsonline.com/news/20180726/new-hanover-task-force-plans-to-deal-with-aces-in-childrens-lives.

9 Patrick Sharkey, "Ending Urban Poverty: The Inherited Ghetto; Understanding the Persistence of Racial Inequality," *Boston Review*, January 1, 2008.

10 Michael Brice-Saddler, Justin Jouvenal, and Perry Stein, "Trip to an Ice Cream Truck Ends in Bullets," *Washington Post*, July 18, 2018.

11 Jessica Contrera, "Summer Meant Popsicles and Pogo Sticks. Then a 10-Year-Old Was Shot to Death," *Washington Post*, July 21, 2018.

12 David Harris, "Another Sad Truth about Makiyah Wilson's Killing," *Washington Post*, August 2, 2016.

13 Michael Brice-Saddler, "Violence Hits Home in Area Where Gunshots Are Commonplace," *Washington Post*, September 8, 2018.

14 Arthur Kellerman, "Guns for Safety? Dream On, Scalia," *Washington Post*, June 29, 2008.

Chapter 5

1 Mark Thompson, "Unlocking the Secrets of PTSD," *Time*, April 6, 2015, 41–43.

2 Rajiv Chandrasekaren, "A Legacy of Pain and Pride," *Washington Post*, March 29, 2014. Poll conducted by the *Washington Post* and the Kaiser Foundation.

3   Becky Fogel, "Understanding the Epidemic of Gun Violence," December 4, 2015, *Science Friday*, podcast, 12:10.

4   Richard Reeves and Sarah Holmes, "Guns and Race: The Different Worlds of Black and White Americans," Brookings Institute: Social Mobility Memos, December 15, 2015.

5   Anne Manning, "Why White, Older Men Are More Likely to Die of Suicide," Colorado State University Public Paper, January 30, 2016.

6   Joshua Cohen, "'Diseases of Despair' Contribute to Declining U.S. Life Expectancy," *Forbes*, July 19, 2018, https://www.forbes.com/sites/joshuacohen/2018/07/19/diseases-of-despair-contribute-to-declining-u-s-life-expectancy/.

7   "Duration of Suicidal Crises ," Harvard School of Public Health, accessed May 1, 2019, https://www.hsph.harvard.edu/means-matter/means-matter/duration/.

8   American Association of Suicidology, "Survivors of Suicide Fact Sheet" (2014).

9   "Means Matter," Harvard School of Public Health, accessed May 1, 2019, https://www.hsph.harvard.edu/means-matter.

10   Joseph Westermeyer, "Firearms, Legislation, and Suicide Prevention," *American Journal of Public Health* 74, no. 2. (February 1984): 108.

11   Richard Seiden, "Where Are They Now? A Follow-up Study of Suicide Attempters from the Golden Gate Bridge," *Suicide and Life Threatening Behavior* 8, no. 4 (Winter 1978): 2.

12   Lenny Bernstein, "Five States Allow Guns to Be Seized before Someone Can Commit Violence," *Washington Post*, February 16, 2018.

13   Patricia Dischinger, Gabriel Ryb, J. A. Kufera, and S. M. Ho, "Declining Statewide Trends in Motor Vehicle Crashes and Injury-Related Hospital Admissions," *Annals of Advances in Automotive Medicine* 57 (September 2013): 247–48.

14   Madeline Drexler, "Guns and Suicide: The Hidden Toll," *Harvard School of Public Health Magazine*, December 4, 2014.

15   Courtney Love (speech, Million Mom March, Washington, DC, May 14, 2000).

16   Cited by Dan Keating, "A Striking Racial Divide in Deaths by Firearms," *Washington Post*, March 24, 2013.

17   Ibid.

18   Ibid.

19   Ibid.

Chapter 6

1   David Sedaris, "Active Shooter," *New Yorker*, July 9 and 16, 2018.

2   John Woodrow Cox and Steven Rich, "Scarred by School Shootings," *Washington Post*, March 25, 2018.

3 Editorial Board, "Erasing Guns from Gun Violence," *Washington Post*, June 8, 2018.

4 Laura Meckler and Moriah Balingit, "Betsy DeVos Considers Allowing Schools to Use Federal Funds to Buy Guns," *Washington Post*, August 23, 2018, https://www.washingtonpost.com/news/grade-point/wp/2018/08/23/betsy-devos-considers-allowing-schools-to-use-federal-funds-to-buy-guns/.

5 John Woodrow Cox and Steven Rich, "The Gun's Not in the Closet," *Washington Post*, August 5, 2018.

6 Ibid.

7 Arwa Mahdawi, "Sacha Baron Cohen's Scheme to Arm Toddlers Isn't Far from Reality," *The Guardian*, July 16, 2018, https://www.theguardian.com/us-news/2018/jul/16/sacha-baron-cohen-guns-children-toddlers-who-is-america-reality.

8 Tom Dart, "University of Texas Professor Quits over State's Campus Carry Law," *The Guardian*, October 8, 2015.

9 "NYPD: 9 Shooting Bystander Victims Hit by Police Gunfire," Fox News, August 25, 2012, https://www.foxnews.com/us/nypd-9-shooting-bystander-victims-hit-by-police-gunfire.

10 Julia Dahl, "Empire State Building Shooting Sparks Questions about NYPD Shot Accuracy," CBS News, August 29, 2012, https://www.cbsnews.com/news/empire-state-building-shooting-sparks-questions-about-nypd-shot-accuracy/.

11 "Arm Teachers? The Facts Argue against It," Violence Policy Center, February 23, 2018, http://vpc.org/press/violence-policy-center-backgrounder-arm-teachers-the-facts-argue-against-it/.

12 Christopher Ingraham, "For Many Mass Shooters Armed Guards Aren't a Deterrent; They're Part of the Fantasy," *Washington Post*, March 1, 2018.

13 Ibid.

14 Ibid.

15 Christopher Ingraham, "In the Past Five Years at Least Six Americans Have Been Shot by Dogs," *Washington Post*, October 27, 2015.

16 "Dear Ann," *Washington Post*, May 23, 2001.

17 Mike Fannen, "Flush Arrogant Gun Policy," *Kansas City (MO) Star*, September 25, 2013.

18 Luz Lazo and Greg Miller, "Ex-Official with CIA Arrested at BWI," *Washington Post*, August 8, 2015.

19 Dana Hedgpeth, "TSA Confiscated Nearly 4,000 Guns at Airport Checkpoints in 2017," *Washington Post*, January 30, 2018.

20 Alana Abramson, "Florida Didn't Conduct Gun Background Checks for a Year Because an Employee Couldn't Log In," *Fortune*, June 8, 2018.

21 Bob Herbert, "A Culture Soaked in Blood," *New York Times*, April 24, 2009.

22 Maxine Bernstein, "Gunman Gets 13 Years for Shooting over Mix-Up on Order at McDonald's," *Oregonian*, December 11, 2003.

23   Tarek El-Tablawy, "Gunman with a Grudge Kills Ex-friend in Church Service," Associated Press, March 31, 2003.

24   Associated Press, "Barr Nearly a Victim of His Own Beliefs," Fox News, August 7, 2002, https://www.foxnews.com/story/barr-nearly-a-victim-of -his-own-beliefs.

25   Bill Vidonic, "Police: Man Accidently Fired Gun Twice," *Beaver County Times* (Beaver, PA), August 22, 2002.

26   "Girl Critically Hurt after Being Shot in the Eye with BB Gun," WANE.com, January 4, 2017, https://www.wane.com/news/local-news/ person-critically-hurt-from-airsoft-gun-shot/1035678995.

27   Herbert Lowe, "A Deadly Discovery," *Newsday*, July 2, 2001.

28   Christian Davenport, "Son, 3, Wounded by Gun of Secret Service Officer," *Washington Post*, June 9, 2001.

29   Caitlyn Keating, "Father Fatally Shoots 9-Year-Old Daughter while Teaching His Sons about Gun Safety: 'I Thought It Was Empty,'" *People*, June 30, 2017.

30   Chuck Shepherd, "Bible-Quoting Contest: Loser Shoots. Kills Winner," Associated Press, July 18, 1996. Cited in James E. Atwood, *America and Its Guns: A Theological Exposé* (Eugene, OR: Cascade Books, 2012), 8.

31   Kenneth Reich, "Police Issue Holiday Reminder," *Los Angeles Times*, December 29, 2001.

32   David Bartowiak Jr., "Detroit Police: Man Throws Shoe with Gun in It at Cockroach, Bullet Strikes Him in Foot," Click On Detroit, March 19, 2019.

33   Eric Nagourney, "Caps on Outlets, but No Locks for Guns," *New York Times*, May 15, 2001.

34   Samantha Raphelson, "How Often Do People Use Guns in Self-Defense?," NPR's *Here and Now*, April 13, 2018.

Chapter 7

1   Petula Dvorak, "We Can't Afford the True Cost of Gun Crime," *Washington Post*, April 13, 2012.

2   Ibid.

3   Mary Ellen Godin, "Take a Look at the New $50 Million Sandy Hook Elementary School in Newtown, Connecticut," Business Insider, July 29, 2016, https://www.businessinsider.com/sandy-hook-elementary-new -school-newtown-connecticut-2016-7.

4   Scott Martelle, "We All Pay: The High Costs of Gun Violence," *Los Angeles Times*, April 17, 2015.

5   Mark Follman et al., "The True Cost of Gun Violence in America: The Data the NRA Doesn't Want You to See," *Mother Jones*, April 15, 2015.

6   Kim Parker et al., *America's Complex Relationship with Guns* (Washington, DC: Pew Research Center, 2017), https://www .pewsocialtrends.org/2017/06/22/guns-and-daily-life-identity-experiences -activities-and-involvement/#dangerous-encounters-with-guns-vary-by

-gun-ownership-key-demographics.

7   Bob Herbert, "A Culture Soaked in Blood," *New York Times*, April 24, 2009.

8   This fifty-five-minute documentary is available through the Presbyterian Church (USA) at 800-728-7228 and at https://pda.pcusa.org/pda/resource/dvd-trigger/.

9   Tim Jones and John McCormick, "Chicago Killings Cost $2.5 Billion as Murders Top N.Y.'s," Bloomberg, May 22, 2013, https://www.bloomberg.com/news/articles/2013-05-23/first-lady-s-chicago-shows-gun-toll-for-city-that-bleeds.

10   Follman et al., "The True Cost."

11   "One in 31 U.S. Adults Are behind Bars, on Parole, or on Probation," Pew Charitable Trust, March 2, 2009.

12   Michelle Ye Hee Lee, "Does the United States Really Have 5 Percent of the World's Population and One-Quarter of the World's Prisoners?," *Washington Post*, April 30, 2015.

13   "Highest to Lowest—Prison Population Total," World Prison Brief, accessed April 29, 2019, http://www.prisonstudies.org/highest-to-lowest/prison-population-total.

14   James E. Atwood, *Gundamentalism and Where It Is Taking America* (Eugene, OR: Wipf and Stock, 2017), 174.

15   Karl Menninger, "The Crime of Punishment," *This Week*, March 23, 1969.

16   Ibid.

Chapter 8

1   Natalie O'Neill, "Cop Fatally Shoots Security Guard at Bar in Chicago Suburbs," *New York Post*, November 18, 2018.

2   Bill Hutchison, "My Son Was Murdered Says Father of Man Mistakenly Shot by Police," ABC News, December 3, 2018.

3   Brock's name and this quote are on display in Mattocks Hall in Tryon Palace, New Bern, NC.

4   "What Is the Doctrine of Discovery?," Dismantling the Doctrine of Discovery, accessed April 24, 2019, https://dofdmenno.org/.

5   Brandon Weber, "How African American WWII Veterans Were Scorned by the G.I. Bill," *The Progressive*, November 10, 2017, https://progressive.org/dispatches/how-african-american-wwii-veterans-were-scorned-by-the-g-i-b/.

6   Nick Kotz, "'When Affirmative Action Was White': Uncivil Rights," *New York Times Book Review*, August 28, 2005.

7   Ibid.

8   Cited in ibid.

9   Manning Marabel, *Race, Reform, and Rebellion: The Second Reconstruction in Black America, 1945–1990* (Oxford, MI: University Press of Mississippi, 1991), 44.

10 James H. Cone, *The Cross and the Lynching Tree* (Ossining, NY: Orbis Books, 2011), xiv.

11 Gurdon Brewster, *No Turning Back: My Summer with Daddy King* (Maryknoll, NY: Orbis, 2011), 163.

12 Thomas Byrne Edsall and Mary Edsall, *Chain Reaction: The Impact of Race, Rights, and Taxes on American Politics* (New York: Norton, 1992), 12–13, cited in Michelle Alexander, *The New Jim Crow: Mass Incarceration in the Age of Colorblindness* (New York: New Press, 2011), 46.

13 Vesla Weaver, "Frontlash: Race and the Development of Punitive Crime Policy," *Studies in American Political Development* 21, no. 2 (Fall 2007): 259.

14 Michelle Alexander, *The New Jim Crow: Mass Incarceration in the Age of Colorblindness* (New York: New Press, 2011), 40.

15 Dan Baum, "Legalize It All: How to Win the War on Drugs," *Harper's*, April 2016.

16 "War on Drugs," History, last modified August 21, 2018, https://www.history.com/topics/crime/the-war-on-drugs.

17 Alexander, *The New Jim Crow*, 57. Alexander cites Loïc Wacquant, "Class, Race, and Hyperincarceration in Revanchist America," *Daedalus* 28, no. 3 (2014): 77.

18 Gwen Sharp, "Black/White Disparities in Prison Sentences," The Society Pages, August 2, 2008, https://thesocietypages.org/socimages/2008/08/02/blackwhite-disparities-in-prison-sentences/.

19 Alexander, *The New Jim Crow*, 51, 112, 7.

20 Ibid., 6. Alexander cites Pew Center on the States, *One in 100: Behind Bars in America 2008* (Washington, DC: Pew Charitable Trusts, 2008), 5.

21 John Granlich, "The Gap between the Number of Blacks and Whites in Prison Is Shrinking," Pew Research Center, January 12, 2018.

22 Alexander, *The New Jim Crow*, 13.

23 Ibid., 51. Alexander cites, among others, Glenn Greenwald, *Drug Decriminalization in Portugal: Lessons for Creating Fair and Successful Drug Policies* (Cato Institute: Washington, DC, 2009); Susan Glaser, "Dutch Cut Overdose Deaths by Dispensing Pure Heroin," *The Plain Dealer* (Cleveland, OH), July 15, 2018.

24 Alexander, *The New Jim Crow*, 180.

25 David Cole, *No Equal Justice: Race and Class in the American Criminal Justice System* (New York: The New Press, 1999), 47. Cited in ibid., 71.

26 Alexander, *The New Jim Crow*, 71. Alexander cites the Florida Department of Highway Safety and Motor Vehicles, Office of General Counsel, *Common Characteristics of Drug Couriers* (1984), sec. I.A.4.

27 Cone, *Cross and the Lynching Tree*, 163.

28 Breea Willingham, "Black Women's Prison Narratives and the Intersection of Race, Gender, and Sexuality in U.S. Prisons," *Critical Survey* 23, no. 3 (2011): 56.

29 Victoria Law, "Invisibility of Women Prisoner Resistance," Women and Prison, May 13, 2010, http://womenandprison.org/social-justice/view/invisibility_of_women_prisoner_resistance/.

30 Michael Cohen, "How For-Profit Prisons Have Become the Biggest Lobby No One Is Talking About," *Washington Post*, April 28, 2015.

31 Ibid.

32 Ibid.

33 Steven Elbow, "Hooked on SWAT: Fueled with Drug Enforcement Money, Military-Style Police Teams Are Exploding in the Backwoods of Wisconsin," *Madison Capital Times*, August 18, 2001.

34 Peter Wagner and Bernadette Rabuy, "Following the Money of Mass Incarceration," Prison Policy Initiative, January 25, 2017, www.prisonpolicy.org/reports/money.html.

35 Dahleen Glanton, "Growing up with Poverty and Violence: A North Lawndale Teen's Story," *Chicago Tribune*, August 21, 2018.

36 Alexander, *The New Jim Crow*, 2.

37 Ibid.

38 Brian Thompson, "The Racial Wealth Gap: Addressing America's Most Pressing Epidemic," *Forbes*, February 18, 2018, https://www.forbes.com/sites/brianthompson1/2018/02/18/the-racial-wealth-gap-addressing-americas-most-pressing-epidemic/.

39 Richard Florida, "How Poor Americans Get Exploited by Their Landlords," CityLab, March 21, 2019.

40 Cited in Gun Violence Policy Group, "Gun Violence: In the Inner City," Harvard Law School, November 26, 2013, http://learning.law.harvard.edu/frontiertorts/topics/inner-city-gun-violence/.

41 Michael Planty and Jennifer L. Truman, *Firearm Violence, 1993–2011* (Washington, DC: U.S. Department of Justice, 2013), 5.

42 Gun Violence Policy Group, "Gun Violence."

43 Mark Guarino, "Shooting Survivors Unite in Chicago to Address Gun Violence," *Washington Post*, June 18, 2018.

44 Josh Horwitz, "The Racial Double Standard on Gun Violence," *Huffington Post*, December 9, 2014, https://www.huffpost.com/entry/the-racial-double-standar_b_5957816.

45 Ibid.

46 Ibid.

47 Quoted in Michael Scherer and Elizabeth Dias, "Trayvon," *Time*, July 29, 2013, 12.

48 Josh Horwitz, "The Shootings That Aren't Trending," *Huffington Post*, July 15, 2016.

49 Eric Holder Jr., "Attorney General Eric Holder at the Department of Justice African American History Month Program" (speech, Washington, DC, February 18, 2009). Emphasis added.

50 *Webster's New World College Dictionary*, 5th ed. (2014), s.v. "privilege"; "white privilege."

51 Krishnadev Calamur, "S.C. Dashcam Video: A Broken Tail Light, a Routine Traffic Stop, a Fleeing Man," NPR, April 9, 2015.

52 Jamilah Pitts, "Don't Say Nothing: Silence Speaks Volumes. Our Students Are Listening," *Teaching Tolerance* 54 (Fall 2016), 47–49.

53 Ibid.

Chapter 9

1 U.S. Department of Defense, "Department of Defense (DoD) Releases Fiscal Year 2017 President's Budget Proposal," February 9, 2016; U.S. Department of Defense, "DoD Releases FY 2018 Budget Proposal," May 23, 2017.

2 Kimberly Amadeo, "U.S. Military Budget: Its Components, Challenges, and Growth: Why Military Spending Is More Than You Think It Is," The Balance, March 12, 2019, https://www.thebalance.com/u-s-military-budget -components-challenges-growth-3306320.

3 Walter Wink, *Engaging the Powers: Discernment and Resistance in a World of Domination*, reprint ed. (Minneapolis: Fortress Press, 1992), 23, 22.

4 Wayne LaPierre (speech, Conservative Political Action Conference, Washington, DC, February 27, 2009).

5 Francis Clines, "When Ronald Reagan Embraced Gun Control," *New York Times*, October 8, 2015.

6 Todd C. Frankel, "Why the CDC Still Isn't Researching Gun Violence, Despite the Ban Being Lifted Two Years Ago," *Washington Post*, January 14, 2105, https://www.washingtonpost.com/news/storyline/wp/2015/01/14/ why-the-cdc-still-isnt-researching-gun-violence-despite-the-ban-being -lifted-two-years-ago/.

7 Ibid.

8 Samantha Raphelson, "How the NRA Worked to Stifle Gun Violence," NPR's *Here and Now Compass*, April 5, 2018.

9 Dylan Scott, "We Aren't Having an Evidence-Based Debate about Guns," Vox, February 28, 2018, https://www.vox.com/policy-and-politics/ 2018/2/28/17058236/gun-control-research-parkland-shooting.

10 Laura Wexler, "Gun Shy: How a Lack of Funds Translates to Inadequate Research on Gun Violence in America," *Public Health*, Fall 2017, https:// magazine.jhsph.edu/2017/fall/features/cassandra-crifasi-hopkins -moderate-gun-owner-gun-policy-researcher/how-the-dickey-amendment -affects-gun-violence-research.html.

11 Mayors against Illegal Guns, *Access Denied: How the Gun Lobby Is Depriving Police, Policy Makers, and the Public the Data We Need to Prevent Gun Violence* (New York: Everytown for Gun Safety, 2013), http:// everytown.org/wp-content/uploads/2014/04/AccessDenied.pdf.

12   Scott, "We Aren't Having."

13   Steven Novella, "Gun Violence as a Public Health Issue," Science-Based Medicine, February 21, 2018, https://sciencebasedmedicine.org/gun-violence-as-a-public-health-issue/.

14   Kate Irby, "With Resources Scarce, ATF Struggles to Inspect Gun Dealers," McClatchy, January 8, 2018, https://www.mcclatchydc.com/news/nation-world/national/article193268134.html.

15   Tana Ganeva and Laura Gottesdeiner, "Nine Terrifying Facts about America's Biggest Police Force," Salon, September 28, 2012, https://www.salon.com/2012/09/28/nine_terrifying_facts_about_americas_biggest_police_force/.

16   Irby, "With Resources Scarce."

17   Narjas Zatat, "There Are More Gun Shops in the U.S. Than Starbucks, McDonalds and Supermarkets Put Together," Indy100, June 16, 2016, https://www.indy100.com/article/there-are-more-gun-shops-in-the-us-than-starbucks-mcdonalds-and-supermarkets-put-together--W1NPIvYg84b.

18   Irby, "With Resources Scarce."

19   Christopher Ingraham, "New Evidence Confirms What Gun Rights Advocates Have Said for a Long Time about Crime," *Washington Post*, July 27, 2016.

20   Natalie Pompilio, "States with Weak Firearm Laws Lead in Crime Gun Exports," *Philadelphia Daily News*, September 28, 2010; Firearms Loophole Closing Act, H.R. 4342, 115th Congress (2017).

21   "Sorry State of Gun Control," editorial, *New York Times*, October 31, 2010; "Background Check Procedures," Giffords Law Center, accessed May 15, 2019, https://lawcenter.giffords.org/gun-laws/policy-areas/background-checks/background-check-procedures/.

22   U.S. Department of Justice Office of the Inspector General, *Review of ATF's Federal Firearms Licensee Inspection Program* (Washington, DC: Department of Justice, 2003), https://oig.justice.gov/reports/2013/e1305.pdf.

23   Bureau of Alcohol, Tobacco and Firearms, *Commerce Firearms in the United States* (Washington, DC: Department of the Treasury, 2000), 2.

24   Allison Graves, "Do 1 Percent of Gun Sellers Supply More Than Half of All the Guns Used in Crimes?," PolitiFact, March 16, 2018, https://www.politifact.com/florida/statements/2018/mar/16/cory-booker/are-1-percent-gun-retailers-responsible-more-half-/.

25   Sari Horwitz and James V. Grimaldi, "AFT's Oversight Limited in Face of Gun Lobby," *Washington Post*, October 26, 2010.

26   Ibid. Emphasis added.

27   For further examination of America's absurd gun laws, see chapter 15 of my book *America and Its Guns*, entitled "Fifty Laws and Policies That Perpetuate Murder and Disorder."

28   Joshua Horwitz, letter from the Executive Director of the Coalition to Stop Gun Violence to the Organization, March 25, 2019.

29 Kimberly Leonard, "Should Doctors Ask about Gun Ownership?," *U.S. News and World Report*, May 17, 2016, https://www.usnews.com/news/ articles/2016-05-17/doctors-should-ask-patients-about-gun-ownership -article-says.

30 Renee Butkus et al., "Reducing Firearm Injuries and Deaths in the United States: A Position Paper from the American College of Physicians," *Annals of Internal Medicine* 169, no. 10 (November 20, 2018).

31 Frances Sellers, "Doctors Fight Back, Share Stories after NRA Tells Them 'To Stay in Their Lane,'" *Washington Post*, November 12, 2018.

32 Paulina Firozi, "Medical Workers May Get Help from Democrats on Stricter Gun Legislation," *Washington Post*, December 4, 2018.

33 Vivian Ho, "Do You Know How Many Bullets I Pull out of Corpses Weekly?—Doctors to NRA," *The Guardian*, November 10, 2018, https:// www.theguardian.com/us-news/2018/nov/09/nra-doctors-tweet-gun -control-deaths.

Chapter 10

1 Quoted in James Rowen, "Guns in Homes Pose Greater Risk to Families Than Intruders, Data Shows," *Milwaukee Journal*, December 20, 2012.

2 Marty Langley and Josh Sugarmann, *Black Homicide Victimization in the U.S.: An Analysis of 2015 Homicide Data* (Washington, DC: Violence Policy Center, 2018), 3.

3 Much of the information in this section comes from Josh Horwitz, "Five Gun Violence Prevention Priorities for the Incoming Congress," *The Hill*, December 13, 2018, https://thehill.com/opinion/civil-rights/421292-five -gun-violence-prevention-priorities-for-the-incoming-congress.

4 Jake Halpern, "The Cop," *New Yorker*, August 10 and 17, 2015, 44–55.

5 Erin Heffernan, "Protesters March for Bail Reform in St. Louis," *St. Louis Post Dispatch*, June 16, 2018.

6 Presbyterian Church (USA) 200th General Assembly (1988), "Statement on Prison Violence and Nonviolent Alternatives," https://www .pcusa.org/resource/restorative-justice/.

7 Beth Avery, "Ban the Box: U.S. Cities, Counties, and States Adopt Fair Hiring Policies," National Employment Law Project, September 25, 2018, https://www.nelp.org/publication/ban-the-box-fair-chance-hiring-state -and-local-guide/.

8 Presbyterian Peace Fellowship, *Gun Violence Prevention Congregational Toolkit*, rev. ed. (Stony Point, NY: Presbyterian Peace Fellowship, 2018), 38, 54.

9 J. Herbert Nelson II, "A Call for More Than Judicial Remedies to the Killing of African American Boys and Men," Presbyterian Church (USA) Office of Public Witness, August 21, 2014, http://pachurchesadvocacy.org/weblog/?p=18918. Written after the killing of Michael Brown in Ferguson, Missouri.

10 Ibid.

Chapter 11

1   Frederick Buechner, *The Hungering Dark* (New York: HarperOne, 1985), 102.

2   Donald B. Kraybill, Steven M. Nolt, and David L. Weaver-Zercher, *Amish Grace: How Forgiveness Transcended Tragedy* (San Francisco: Jossey-Bass, 2007), 46.

3   Abraham Joshua Heschel, "On Prayer" in *Moral Grandeur and Spiritual Audacity: Essays*, ed. Susannah Heschel (New York: Farrar, Straus, and Giroux, 1996), 263.

4   John R. Lewis (commencement speech, Jewish Theological Seminary, New York, May 17, 2013).

5   Presbyterian Church in the United States, "A Declaration of Faith" in *Our Confessional Heritage: Confessions of the Reformed Tradition* (Atlanta: PCUS Materials Distribution Service, 1978), 180.

The Author

JAMES E. ATWOOD is a leader in the faith-based movement against gun violence. He has served as chair of the boards of the Coalition to Stop Gun Violence and Heeding God's Call of Greater Washington, as interfaith coordinator of the Million Mom March, and as a member of the National Committee of the Presbyterian Peace Fellowship. Atwood is the author of *America and Its Guns: A Theological Exposé* and *Gundamentalism and Where It Is Taking America.* His work has been published in *Sojourners, Presbyterian Outlook, Presbyterians Today,* and other publications. Atwood is pastor emeritus of Trinity Presbyterian Church of Arlington, Virginia, and has degrees from Florida State University, Union Theological Seminary (Va.), Princeton Theological Seminary, and McCormick Theological Seminary. He is the recipient of the 2018 David Steele Distinguished Writer Award by the Presbyterian Writers Guild and the 2019 Beard Atwood Award from the Coalition to Stop Gun Violence. He and his wife, Roxana, served as mission workers in Japan from 1965 to 1974 and now live in Harrisonburg, Virginia.